hapusrwydd
onnellisuus
felic...
щастие
lykke
szczęście
felicô
fiafia
bonheur
phúc
happiness
sonas
idunu
fericire
幸福
행복
geluk
lumturi
sreća
шчасце
شادی

IN SEARCH OF
HAPPINESS

IN SEARCH OF
HAPPINESS
FOLLOWING MINDFUL PATHS TO FULFILMENT

MIKE ANNESLEY

WORTH PRESS

First published in 2018
by Worth Press Ltd, Bath, England.
worthpress@btconnect.com

© Worth Press Ltd, 2018

All rights reserved. No part of this publication may be reproduced or transmitted in any form or by any means electronic or mechanical, including photocopying, recording or any information storage and retrieval system, without permission in writing from the publishers.

British Library Cataloguing in Publication Data.
A catalogue record for this book is available from the British Library.

ISBN: 978-1-84931-156-4

10 9 8 7 6 5 4 3 2 1

Publisher's Note: While every effort has been made to ensure that the information herein is complete and accurate, the publisher and author make no representations or warranties either expressed or implied of any kind with respect to this book to the reader. Neither the author nor the publisher shall be liable or responsible for any damage, loss or expense of any kind arising out of information contained in this book. The thoughts or opinions expressed in this book represent the personal views of the author and not necessarily those of the publisher. Further, the publisher takes no responsibility for third party websites or their content.

Editorial Direction: Cristina Galimberti
Design and illustrations: Arati Devasher, aratidevasher.com

Printed and bound in China

For my father, Colin (1925–2017),
in gratitude for all his love and support

CONTENTS

Introduction	9
What is Happiness?	10
A Happiness Toolkit	18
Hygge	32
Positive Psychology	64

Lykke	86
Ikigai	118
Lagom	140
Tibetan Buddhism	168
Further Reading & Index	190

"Happiness consists more in the small conveniences or pleasures that occur every day, than in great pieces of good fortune that happen but seldom to a man in the course of his life."

Benjamin Franklin

INTRODUCTION

Am I happy? I believe so. Do I have issues to address? Definitely. Am I addressing them? Not at the moment, though writing this book has helped me focus on what those issues are and how to start tackling them. I am committed to doing so.

Having a purpose is well known to be one of the most reliable sources of happiness. I have been writing away, focusing in the moment. Alongside that I have been processing a recent big experience.

Three months ago my father died, aged 92. I have no siblings, and not many relatives. I have not been in a romantic relationship for some years, partly because my energies have been focused on my dad. My emotional nourishment comes from friends. One called me every other day after my loss. Four came to the funeral in the English Midlands, travelling considerable distances to do so. The night before, I took three of them to a pub that has not changed since the 1970s. We were the only occupants of the 'snug' – the smarter of two public rooms. The landlord told us the pub's history. Then we went back to the house and I cooked dinner. It was a good evening. The funeral felt good too, in a sad but fulfilling way. I enjoyed the wake, in a village farmhouse my father's grandfather used to own, now a part-time teashop. If this sounds unsentimental, it is. I had already come to accept the inevitability of change, and my father's need for release.

Actually, for many years, I have felt fortunate. I was made redundant from my publishing job in 2013, and this enabled me to spend weeks at a time with Dad, doing the things we enjoyed together.

Between my freelance commissions I wrote a long prose poem, loosely based on the *I Ching*, and self-published it. I hope I will one day connect with a few appreciative readers – there must surely be some, somewhere. I hope I will carry on writing both poetry and mind-body-spirit titles, and find some success with both, at least on the creative level.

I am grateful, hopeful, and ready for new experiences – after being, for several years, a part-time carer. I would say I am happy – not least because I know I have been lucky. I think everyone can find their happiness somewhere in how things are, or how they might be, even if the former takes a bit of a search and the latter a willingness to change.

– Mike Annesley, 2018

CHAPTER ONE

WHAT IS HAPPINESS?

Aristotle argued that happiness is not a state of mind but a disposition — a propensity to live the best life we can, in accord with our values. Many would agree that love is perhaps the greatest value of all. The World Happiness Report, briefly described on page 17, suggests that social factors may provide a background conducive to happiness. But ultimately it is down to the individual to find his or her own way, with guidance from some of the best thinking from cultural traditions and psychology.

THE HAPPINESS QUEST

DESTINATION OR JOURNEY?
The question 'Are you happy?' is not always easy to answer. The answer will often be doubtful or qualified. 'Maybe' can seem the most honest response. Why should there be any uncertainty?

One possible reason is that the questioner has not given us time to process our thoughts. Perhaps we need to do a mental check on the various dimensions of our life — home, family, relationships, work, money, leisure — and come up with an outcome that averages the highs and lows. We are possibly sometimes very happy, at other times less so.

THE ULTIMATE END
Happiness is a baseline, in the sense that we cannot go deeper and ask *why* we are seeking it — though most of us are. It is an end, not a means. It is ingrained in our nature to wish to be happy. Yet we all choose different routes for attaining this state.

This metaphor of travel is appropriate, since many of our satisfactory highlights in life come from attaining our goals; and moving towards a goal is a journey. Most of life, however, is more about seeking than attaining. It is often said that happiness is to be experienced while looking for something, rather than finding it. Could that 'something' be happiness itself? In practice, many people who are happy did not set their sights on happiness but have found it in pursuing whatever purpose has revealed itself to them — to start a family or a business, to devote themselves to doing good, to write a novel or become an inspiring teacher or skilful metalworker. Two traditions of happiness described in this book emphasize purpose as the key to a happy life: *ikigai* (pages 118–139) and positive psychology (pages 64–85).

Happiness is a baseline. We cannot go deeper and ask why we are seeking it.

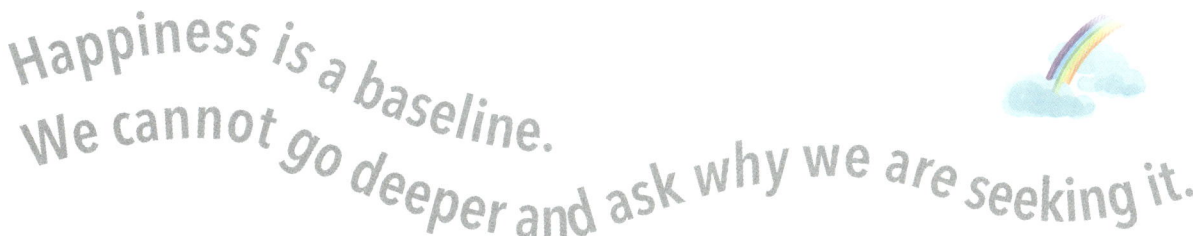

Happiness and pleasure

One person might be happiest walking in the hills, another racing a battered car around a dirt track. One individual might love going to the bowling alley with half a dozen friends, another finds more satisfaction watching a box set on TV with just their partner. All these examples have something in common: each of these four people is engaged in an *activity*. But according to one convincing view of happiness, an activity can give *pleasure*, but only while that activity is continuing. Happiness, by contrast, is longer-lasting. A full life will usually be made of episodes of both pleasure and pain, some of the latter undertaken willingly – for example, when you visit a terminally ill friend in hospital. Happiness, it could be said, is something that can accommodate both extremes.

HAPPINESS, GOODNESS AND LOVE

LIVING WELL

The ancient Greek philosopher Aristotle, who lived more than 2,000 years ago, offers readers of his *Nicomachean Ethics* a view of happiness that is universally and timelessly relevant. Aristotle believed the purpose of human life is to be happy. More interesting than this, however, is his idea that happiness is not a state of mind, like melancholy or hopefulness or pleasure. Instead, it is the ultimate value of your life up to the moment of assessment. You are happy if you have been fulfilling, and are continuing to fulfil, your potential for living well.

Human beings differ from animals in being able to reason. Our mental faculties enable us to set and attain our goals and overcome the challenges by taking considered action. Pleasure alone can never make us happy, since pleasure is what animals seek, and we are better than animals: we have nobler capacities, which we must exercise if we are to make the best of our lives. Instead of blindly following our appetites, we are better served by channelling them in ways appropriate to our elevated status within the natural world.

HAPPINESS FROM WITHIN

The following passage from the *Nicomachean Ethics* expresses an Aristotelean view that many who have thought deeply about happiness would agree with:

> "The function of a human being is to live a certain kind of life, and this implies a rational principle. The role of a good person is the noble performance of this goal. If any action is well performed, it is performed in accord with the appropriate excellence. If this is so, then happiness turns out to be an activity of the soul in accordance with virtue."

Human flourishing depends on how we conduct ourselves, rather than on the blessings that come our way by birth or luck. If we are lucky enough we might possess inherited wealth; or, more likely, we might live in a country where we have freedom and a state welfare system. These things are a buffer against discomfort of varying degrees but do not protect against unhappiness. You can lose your freedom and your welfare entitlement but still manage to find joy – for example, in a birth or birthday – and even, over the longer term, happiness.

If happiness were dependent on external circumstances, it would always be precarious, since misfortune can rob us of any material comfort at any time. A happiness that stems from individual effort – to live by your values, to be good and strive to be better – is more reliable.

Pleasure alone can never make us happy, since pleasure is what animals seek and we are better than animals.

LOVE AND HAPPINESS

To live authentically, compassionately and generously and to cultivate love is to have life in abundance. The Greeks had a particular word for the open-hearted, outgoing kind of love: they called it *agape*. This is not a state of mind but a practice: the habit of giving with no expectation of personal benefit. Some people would say that love and happiness are two sides of one coin. Happiness is the well-being that stems from fully exercising your power to live by your best values; love is the same thing perceived in terms not just of yourself but of your relation to others.

Many traditions of happiness around the world emphasize the importance of human connection – including the Danish emphasis on sharing *hygge* (comfort and warmth) with family and friends; the findings by positive psychologists that loving, caring contact can make you not only happier but healthier; and the premium placed in Buddhism on being selflessly compassionate.

In an intimate relationship, love means that we create for each other the conditions for flourishing. The wedding vow's reference to being there for each other in sickness and in health is embodied for real in countless examples, with one partner selflessly caring for another. A cynic might see such a commitment as the ultimate insurance policy – a hedge against lonely decrepitude. But seen from the inside, the love that compels such self-sacrifice has its own irresistible compulsion, as an instinctive gesture of the heart.

Love means that we create for each other the conditions for flourishing.

HAPPINESS AROUND THE WORLD

TAKING SOUNDINGS

Between 2012 and 2018 six World Happiness Reports have been published, ranking more than 150 countries by the levels of happiness discovered there. Increasingly, happiness is seen as an apt measure of social progress and the goal of public policy. Hopefully, this is a gathering trend.

The 2017 report has these 10 countries, from the happiest downwards, at the top of the survey's life satisfaction ladder: Finland, Norway, Denmark, Iceland, Switzerland, Netherlands, Canada, New Zealand, Australia, Sweden. The USA stands at 18, the UK at 19.

The inclusion in this book of two Nordic happiness concepts – hygge and lagom (lykke, which is also given a chapter, is not a concept but a set of research findings) – reflects the high ranking of Scandinavian countries. Japan's rating is 54, despite the popularity of ikigai (purpose) as a compass for everyday living.

Happy societies

The World Happiness Report is based on self-assessment by individuals, but differences in the findings from one country to another are speculatively explained by looking at some key social variables: GDP per capita. Life expectancy. Social support. Trust in government. Freedom to make life decisions. Generosity (assessed by level of charitable donations).

It may be true that the happiest societies are governed honestly, compassionately and fairly. However, in many countries where this book will find its readership, the social conditions, while far from ideal, will be such that personal happiness is readily available to those prepared to think realistically and honestly about their attitudes, their values and the life choices available to them.

CHAPTER TWO

A HAPPINESS TOOLKIT

Anyone seeking to increase their level of life satisfaction needs to start with a measure of self-understanding. Resilience and flexibility are helpful too, as instruments for dealing with change — both the ups and downs of fortune and the transformations we might choose to put in place to maximize our personal potential. Mindfulness meditation is an effective vehicle for attaining all three of these qualities.

WHERE TO START?

SEARCHING WITHIN AND WITHOUT

Everybody who thinks they would like to be happier has the capacity to be so. But where to start? This is not an easy question to answer, but some general guidelines can be given.

There is no substitute for taking an honest look at yourself, your feelings and your circumstances. You need to be unflinching. You must also be prepared to accept your own part in any aspect of your life that does not feel wholly satisfactory. If you are worried about the quality of your relationship, for example, could it be that this is more to do with your own attitude than with any perceived failings in your partner? Taking responsibility for the situations in which you find yourself is a helpful first step on the road to greater fulfilment.

> "Happiness is not something ready made. It comes from your own actions."
>
> *The 14th Dalai Lama*

> "What a wonderful life I've had. I only wish I'd realized it sooner."
>
> *Colette*

TAKING CHARGE

Frustration is the feeling that what should be happening in your life is not happening, and/or what should not be is. A common response to frustration is to waste mental and emotional energy on blame – directed to people or situations, or both, or to fortune. It is a short step from here to feeling victimized by the powers that be, the forces of destiny that rule your life. The problem with victimhood is that it is passive, and passivity is never a viable way to feel better about life. Good things come only to those who take appropriate action.

Such action will usually involve changes in the way you go about things. However, these changes will tend to spring from a decision – which needs to be strengthened into a commitment. Many life-changing decisions are quite straightforward. An example would be deciding to accept someone with all their peculiarities, rather than wishing they were different. Straightforward decisions – how to behave, how not to behave – can be difficult, requiring strength of character to turn them into commitments. Inner work is the key to success. What could be more important than making a change that will make your happier? Reminding yourself of what is at stake is vital if you are to live by your best choices.

THE GRAVITY OF FRUSTRATION

Unhappiness often has a field of gravity around it – a set of forces that prevent you from breaking out into a new orbit. This may seem contrary to common sense. We all know of people who reach a point in their frustrations when they simply have to make a change: unhappiness is the prompt. Often, though, dissatisfaction is addictive. We stay within its comfort zone of discontent, since taking a viable exit route seems more uncomfortable still.

'Seems' is the key word here, because in fact exchanging a known negative for an unknown positive is always going to result in a net positive. Unfamiliarity is not a true negative: familiarity is not a true positive.

Your relationship with work

If you think of yourself as having a vocation, the whole question of meaning in life probably becomes more straightforward. However, many people have mixed feelings about work and struggle to find true meaning there, even if they show aptitude in their occupation. The life/work balance – in other words, the competing claims of your professional and family lives upon your time – is another common source of inner tension. If you feel that work is compromising your quality of life, consider the following main options:

Changing your job – for example, in terms of time commitment or responsibilities.

Changing your employer – for example, for the sake of a shorter commute or a more supportive environment.

Changing your profession – perhaps to utilize your skills (aptitude) or make a more valuable contribution (meaning) or do something you enjoy (pleasure).

Meaning

+

Aptitude

+

Pleasure

=

Happiness

DIMENSIONS OF CHANGE

In assessing your level of fulfilment, and where you might be able to make useful changes in life to bring more happiness within your reach, it is helpful to think in terms of three broad areas: meaning, aptitude and pleasure. Both meaning and aptitude give purpose, while pleasure might be seen as the reward you claim for being committed to such purpose.

Meaning
Drawing upon your best qualities in order to live by your values gives meaning to life. This might involve, for example, being strong enough to be unselfish when you need to be a care giver. Or it might be a matter of being honest and fair in a profession where many of your peers are deceitful and grasping. Or doing the best you can for your partner and children.

Aptitude
Knowing what you are good at and channelling these abilities into worthwhile pursuits is profoundly satisfying. It boosts your self-esteem, and that in turn boosts your confidence. It also gives you a valued place in the estimation of others. Moreover, it will often provide you with life-orienting goals as you seek to take your existing abilities further.

Pleasure
The basic pleasures of life include companionship, intimacy and an appreciation of nature, entertainment and the arts. For many people, travel and sport also offer pleasure. Work is pleasurable for some but for others can be problematic in robbing them of time for meaning and aptitude.

PRESSURE POINTS

KEEPING STRESS AT BAY
Stress can be a hidden saboteur, undermining our contentment without our even being aware that it has stowed away surreptitiously in our mindset. Alternatively, we may speak to other people of being under stress, and perhaps be quite voluble on the subject, yet still fail to recognize just how deep and damaging this condition is.

A three-pronged stress strategy

Once you have recognized the harm that stress is causing to your health and happiness, there are three broad fronts you can work on to turn your life around to the positive:

Making lifestyle changes
Possibilities include: taking regular breaks; having holidays; delegating problems; saying 'no' more often; working at home occasionally; better time management.

Adjusting your responses
Possibilities include: setting new priorities; finding humour in absurdity; breaking negative habits (drink, smoking and so on); avoiding blame; ceasing to treat your problems as part of your identity.

Adopting healing disciplines
Possibilities include: meditation; counselling; mindfulness-based stress therapy; yoga; aerobic exercise.

Often it takes a considerable measure of self-awareness to understand the causes of chronic stress. The four most common factors to consider are personality, time management issues, perfectionism and the martyrdom syndrome. Each one requires a different response.

- If you worry about small things and herd your problems together to make one all-enveloping crisis (catastrophizing), you have a predisposition to stress. You will need to do some inner work, with mindful attention (see pages 28–31). Try to detach yourself from your problems and see them in a wider perspective.

- If you feel multiple pressures building, that suggests you are not good at prioritizing and managing your time. Perhaps you need to say 'no' to people more often, rather than taking on extra commitments.

- If you worry about not meeting your own standards, through time pressure, you might be expecting too much of yourself. Sometimes 'adequate' is all that is needed, rather than 'perfect'. Avoid excessive perfectionism, which is often a reflection of underlying self-esteem issues.

- If you believe everyone wants a piece of you, could it be you are taking refuge in blame instead of taking responsibility for your own predicament? You have at least *some* control over any situation: you can choose your own response.

FLEXIBILITY AND RESILIENCE

MANAGING LIFE'S CHANGES

Discontented people often talk of being in a rut. They tend to regret missed chances, to feel left behind by the flow of happiness that others surf. There are many possible reasons for such a negative self-image. One is a reluctance to learn new things or adapt to new situations (for example, digital technology or restructuring at work). Another is fear of change in general.

Without change life becomes stultified. Clinging to the status quo is limiting, for it makes our mindset increasingly fossilized – starved of challenge, excitement, learning, discovery and growth. The only way to break out of the impasse is to overcome anxieties and take some calculated risks. We may not immediately achieve the success we seek, but in trying we will grow in self-knowledge and perhaps acquire some new skills in the process. Embracing change is often an essential requirement for your journey to happiness.

OUT OF THE BLUE

Involuntary change – ageing, separation, joblessness, ill health – poses even greater challenges. Even if we are mentally prepared for a shock, it can take the wind out of our sails. Resilience and flexibility to deal with change is best nurtured in advance, by working on self-understanding and acceptance. Mindfulness practices can provide a method of attaining these qualities. Deeply accepting the reality of impermanence, as Buddhists do, can help to lessen the impact of loss or trauma.

> # The bamboo that bends is stronger than the oak that resists.
>
> *Japanese proverb*

Breaking the hold of the past

Sometimes we acquire habits of emotion. A particular kind of situation develops, and our emotions respond as they always have, automatically, as if reacting to a cue. Psychologists call this common emotional syndrome 'autopilot'. It is autopilot that enables a hurt – even one sustained in childhood – to carry itself over into later life. This is the reason many people are shy, or lacking in confidence, or unwilling to commit to new relationships: they have had a bad experience once, and they fear it will be repeated the next time a similar situation arises. In this way unhappiness can be self-perpetuating. Addictions often set in, to help you avoid confronting the truth about yourself. However, you can be liberated from your emotional habits by:

- Undertaking mindfulness meditation (see pages 28–31).
- Understanding the underlying causes of your automatic responses.
- Refusing to give such responses your permission.
- Creating new positive habits to replace the negative ones.

THE WAY OF MINDFULNESS

LIVING IN THE MOMENT

Mindfulness has in recent decades become established as one of most effective and attractive of all self-help therapeutic disciplines. It is also an easy entry route into meditation.

The American scientist Jon Kabat-Zinn, from the 1970s, conducted an eight-week course of practice which he later relaunched as Mindfulness-Based Stress Reduction (MBSR). His purpose was to help his patients deal with their sources of distress, though simple meditation techniques. A related development was Mindfulness-Based Cognitive Therapy, which has been proven to reduce the incidence of depression.

One of the reasons for the widespread popularity of mindfulness is its promotion as a tool to make us better able to deal with anxiety. In addition, it has irresistible benefits for personal effectiveness – sharpening concentration, improving memory, enhancing communication and helping us deal with our troubling emotions. The implications for happiness are profoundly appealing.

Mindfulness meditation, done regularly over two or three weeks, can break down our habits of thought and emotion and return us to our original openness.

Elements of mindfulness

Mindfulness releases you from fretting about an unknown future and an unchangeable past. Fear and regret are banished by a truer perspective. You are freed to be more fully yourself. The basic components of mindfulness are:

Recognizing your feelings without being caught up in their story.

Discovering your true self, unclouded by anxiety and low self-esteem.

Living more in the present, less in the past and future.

Making free choices rather than repeating past responses over and over.

An apple here and now

This fruit meditation is designed as a basic introduction to mindfulness practice. Repetition is important. After completing the exercise you might go on to try the breathing meditation on page 181 – not just once, but every few days over a period of, say, three weeks. You can substitute any fruit for the apple, or if you prefer you could use a pepper pot, a cup and saucer, or any simple small object. If any thoughts or feelings come into your mind while meditating, be conscious of them but avoid dwelling on them – just return your focus to the apple and let them pass away.

1. Sit at a table with the apple in front of you.
2. Look closely at the apple for about five minutes, noting every aspect of it visually – its shape, its colour, its shadows. Do not think about its taste or its nutritional value, or anything else.
3. Hold the apple in your hands, and turn it around in all directions. Attend to its textures – how it feels as well as how it looks. Put the apple back on the table after a further five minutes or so.
4. Close your eyes and concentrate on your sensations – your breathing, the feel of your clothes, the pressure from the chair.
5. Concentrate next on sound: the rhythm of your breathing, and any ambient noise you can hear.
6. Look back on what you have experienced: that is, a sensory break from your thoughts and emotions. Doing this regularly over time can be deeply refreshing.

PRESENT AWARENESS

The basic principle behind mindfulness meditation is that we displace wandering, anxious thoughts and emotions by focusing fully on an experience in the present moment. This could be our own breathing, or the sensations in our body generally. However, a good starting point for beginners is to meditate on an object, such as an apple or orange. The point is to direct your full attention to that object – its shape, colour, texture, and so on. While performing this practice, most people find their mind will occasionally wander. When this happens, all you do is notice what has happened – *without judging yourself* for it – and gently return your focus to the object.

While doing a mindfulness meditation, you allow yourself to be open-hearted and 'spacious'. That word, which might seem puzzling, refers to purity of mind. Our pure minds acquire habits of thinking and feeling, as a result of accumulated experiences over time. Mindfulness meditation, when done regularly over two or three weeks, can break down these habits and return us to our original openness.

In the process, our sense of who we are and what we can potentially become can change for the better. To follow the path of mindfulness is to be enriched – to live more fully, easily, flexibly and happily. We grow in self-awareness, and can build on that as a foundation for fulfilment. We no longer believe the critic inside our own minds who judges us so harshly – our negative self-talk, as a psychologist would put it. We accept ourselves as we are while committing to make any realistic changes that will make our lives better.

> "To a mind that is still, the whole universe surrenders."
>
> *Lao Tzu*

CHAPTER THREE
HYGGE

How to find happiness by following the Danish principle of hygge, based on warmth, comfort, celebration, friendship, love and mindfully living in the present moment.

HOME AND BEYOND

INTRODUCING HYGGE

If the home is a castle, as folk wisdom has told us from the 16th century and probably earlier, what its imaginary battlements defend is the life we define for ourselves. Within the limits of home we have control over our environment. We can shape our spaces to maximize comfort and convenience – and thereby provide a sympathetic setting for our loving transactions with family and friends. These ideas are at the heart of hygge: the Danish word (pronounced 'hoo-guh') that in recent years has migrated from its northern homeland to provide a fashionable concept of happiness applicable to all.

HEARTH AND HEART

Given the long, cold, snowy Scandinavian winter, it is understandable that Nordic folk have turned inwards towards the hearth. The fire blazing there, with candles all around, and comfortable seating, offers a focus for convivial living and intimate sharing. Around this vision of domestic perfection, ideals of tradition and naturalness also cluster. In turn these ideals branch into a spreading network of key values, all universal, and all indispensable as components of the good life according to hygge: comfort, warmth, purity, simplicity, connection, memory.

Identifying the household as the central hub of happy living does not, of course, restrict happiness to indoors, nor to the coldest season. The hearth is really a symbol of the priorities implied by hygge – an easy way to visualize them. It is also a place – but one of many possible places – that offers scope for their expression.

A note on terminology

'Hygge' is a verb as well as a noun. You can hygge with friends and family, or on your own. The adjective derived from the word is 'hyggeligt', which means it has the capacity to help you hygge.

IN THE MOMENT, WITH OTHERS

The popular perception inevitably simplifies. There is also a more profound, even philosophical, dimension to hygge. The concept could be described as perceiving and appreciating certain kinds of moment as special, regardless of location or season.

This takes us into the realm of mindfulness. Whereas mindfulness meditation practice generally focuses on particular objects or sensations, the hygge style of mindfulness also involves savouring an atmosphere – of comfort, well-being, contentment. In other words, it looks inwards, towards your state of mind.

Hygge sees the good life as comfort, warmth, purity, simplicity, connection, memory.

The state of Denmark

The Danes tend to receive high ratings in international surveys of happiness levels. In 2016 the World Happiness Report rated Denmark the happiest nation in the world, knocking Switzerland off the sweet spot. There are social factors at work here, including free education and healthcare, a high level of gender equality, good income distribution, a tradition of liberal-mindedness and a high level of trust in government. However, a further reason may be the contribution made by hygge to the Danish mindset. The importance attached to warm human connections, and mindfully enjoying the pleasures of home and hearth, have no doubt made Danes less vulnerable to the competitive striving that has often caused unhappiness in more materialistic societies.

Try hygge now

To appreciate the hygge mood, have half a dozen friends or family round to your home for supper. Serve something quick to cook (or maybe cooked in advance) so you can join in the pre-supper drinks. Build the following ingredients into the evening:

Comfort
Maybe use big cushions, or *extra* cushions. Take your time over the drinks and encourage people to relax.

Shadows
Even in summer, use shadows to create atmosphere. Dim the lights or use blinds or spotlighting to dramatize the setting.

Candles
Set candles on the table so their flickering flames create a collection of miniature hearths.

Treats
Chocolates and cake spring to mind, but use your initiative. Offer liqueurs, port or suchlike afterwards.

Nature
Pine cones, seasonal flowers, leaves or fruits, are all suitable mood-boosters.

Nostalgia
Encourage people to talk about what they have enjoyed – including events those particular guests have savoured *together*.

Touch
Hug and touch your guests. Give little pats on the arm, hand or shoulder to reassure and comfort.

However, at the same time, the Danes value being sociable. The atmosphere of hygge can be appreciated on your own but it is in small gatherings that the notion comes into its true realm. In any get-together the values to relish are sharing, kindness, generosity, warmth. All these come to the fore in entertainment; and, indeed, to be hospitable, gathering together like-minded souls for refreshment, is perhaps the easiest way to create the right atmosphere.

Typically hygge

Although hygge is difficult to define precisely, there are certain phenomena that seem saturated in its essence. These include:

Candles	Logs	Tapestry	Baskets
Fragrance	Slippers	Cardigans	Driftwood
Bygones	Snowman	Toboggan	Mulled wine

PLEASURES OF THE HEARTH

BENEFITING FROM LIGHT AND WARMTH

The hearth is the civilized equivalent of the campfire. Originally, as well as being a life-saving source of warmth, a fire was also a gathering place for meals, ceremonies and storytelling. It was where we felt safe, protected from the outer darkness, the unknown. The sense of being quintessentially at home in the familiar centre of our domestic lives is reassuring and fulfilling. Many homes, even in a modernistic style, retain the hearth, at least vestigially, as the focus of our most comfortable waking hours.

Anyone who seeks to bring hygge into their lives is recommended, as a first step, to identify the main 'hearth' of the home. If it is a fireplace, so much the better: you can work on the feature and its immediate surroundings to augment its atmosphere. However, central heating means that many homes have a notional hearth rather than a real one. In this case, do you spend money on reshaping the room and installing a real hearth, or do you make do with visual gestures that simulate the genuine article? A further complication is whether to have a visible fire, whether open on a grate or enclosed in a stove, as your source of heating. Such decisions are down partly to taste, partly to cost.

Hygge never shrinks from a plethora of patterns, since that evokes plenty.

In favour of fire

It may involve considerable expense to create a real fireplace in your home – that is, one with a real fire – but consider this as option. The following advantages will unfold:

Atmosphere
No other form of heating gives you the intimate warmth of a fire. Whether they play in a hearth or a stove, the flames will serve as a prompt for your imagination. You will have a cheerful place to settle with family or friends, pull up a comfortable chair for reading, or enjoy knitting, sewing or listening to the radio.

Romance
The fireside, like the lakeside, is a romantic setting for sharing endearments. Firelight caught in a wineglass has a magic of its own. Parents unable to find a babysitter should consider the hearth as the setting for a wonderful night in.

Back-up supply
Especially in times of winter storms, electricity failure can lead to black-out. Old boilers can fail, shutting down central heating. A fireplace gives you warmth and a measure of light while waiting for normal service to be restored.

Hot food and drink
A wood-burning stove can also be a hotplate for cooking. Heat soup or coffee on the stove in traditional style, saving money on power bills. If you have an open-hearth fireplace, share with others the pleasure of roasting marshmallows on long sticks.

The eco factor
In contrast to fossil fuels, wood is carbon-neutral: it does not produce more CO_2 than is already present in the carbon cycle. Although wood-burning does create particles that can contribute to pollution, you can limit this by burning dry, seasoned wood in a modern eco-friendly stove. Briquettes, made of recycled waste wood, are an even greener fuel.

CUSHIONED COMFORT

Even a minimalist or notional hearth can be imbued with hygge. A well-crafted rug helps emphasize the visual focus while radiating welcome and homeliness. Cushions should ideally be large with patterned covers – hygge never shrinks from a plethora of patterns, evoking plenty. Choose fabrics and ornaments you find aesthetically pleasing, and perhaps with a story behind them – if only the story of your eagerly choosing and buying. Keep the lighting low-key. Use your hearth to relish good company (including your own), happy memories and warm generosity.

> "Don't you love a cushioned seat in a corner, by the fireside, with your slippers on your feet?"
>
> *Oliver Wendell Holmes*

MEANINGFUL OBJECTS

APPRECIATING EVOCATION AND BEAUTY

Objects are lost, or get stolen or broken, and unhappiness lies in being too attached to them, according to Buddhism. However, there is another approach to looking at objects: as cherished things whose history and beauty makes them priceless. True, any object invested with our love can be lost or stolen. But the natural trajectory for ownership of such possessions is to keep them until the time feels right for giving them away. This may be when we are feeling loving and generous; or it may be when we reach our end. It has been said we do not own beautiful things, we hold them in trust for the next generation.

Boxes for giving

The Danes love to give presents in ornamental boxes. Imitate this practice, putting effort into the embellishment to show the gift of your own time as an extra token of affection. Collect unwanted boxes in any material and use them instead of wrapping paper for your gifts to friends and family. Be imaginative in your coverings. Create collage effects or apply handpainting or stencilling. Stick on decorative stars – or perhaps even real or imitation leaves. Wrap your box loosely in plain paper to heighten the surprise.

Sarah's sweater: a hygge case study

The Danish TV detective drama series *Forbrydelsen* (*The Killing*) popularized a type of black-and-white chunky-knit sweater worn by policewoman Sarah Lund. In fact, the sweater was not from mainland Denmark but from the Faroe Islands, which lie between Scotland, Iceland and Norway. The black wool came from hardy local black sheep: no dyeing was applied. You might imagine the garment came from some folksy cottage workshop. In fact, it was knitted to a design created and patented by the manufacturer, the high-end knitwear company Gudrun & Gudrun (G&G), whose base is in the Faroes.

Hygge-philes may find themselves divided over items like this. Many would favour the genuine, uncommercial, traditional article, scorning G&G for putting a sky-high price tag on something that purports to be rooted in tradition. Others might admire the G&G product for its indisputable quality, and have no quarrel with cognoscenti prepared to dig deep into their pockets for their pleasures.

On balance, hygge is in principle anti-brand, anti-globalism. Sweaters bought from craft workshops, or at farmer's markets or, better still, knitted by someone you love, have the greatest value.

EVERYDAY BEAUTY

It is in the spirit of hygge to admire craftsmanship, especially in traditional styles. Mass production is hygge hell; heavenly is the work of skilled artisans working in natural materials and producing quality work you can handle and use every day.

In the mid-20th century Denmark became known for a style of functionalistic design and architecture influenced by the German Bauhaus school. Hygge, however, tends if anything to favour the folk tradition against which this modern functionalism reacted. Comfort takes priority over elegance. The emphasis is often on rusticity. This is not to say, however, that hygge is an exclusively rural phenomenon, since it is adaptable enough to find expression in city apartments – so long as there is somewhere to lounge and relax, and homeliness (not necessarily clutter) prevails over spartan metropolitan chic.

Characteristic of hygge is a leaning towards the natural world in all its rawness – such items as driftwood sculptures, offcuts of polished wood, sprays of berries, collections of shiny horse chestnuts and pebble still-lives. Fresh flowers provide the perfect setting for spring or summer entertaining. Around Christmas the archetypal decoration is the advent wreath, with four candles, one of which is lit in the Sundays leading up to Christmas Eve. Traditionally the wreath is created from spruce twigs with added visual interest from red berries and spruce cones.

Hygge favours the natural world in all its rawness – driftwood sculptures, offcuts of polished wood, pebble still-lives, sprays of berries.

CIRCLES OF LOVE

NURTURING YOUR CONNECTIONS

The conversation may be peppered with familiar jokes or often-heard opinions. Someone may start telling a story everyone has heard before. Yet any gathering of friends or family has the potential for a quality that more than anything else keeps our darkness and demons at bay: human warmth. When this is apparent, who cares about originality?

WARM LOVE

Warmth is a time-honoured blessing, its value transcending our limitations. Love is the ultimate sharing. Where love is present, even a small gesture – a look or a touch – becomes eloquent and precious. The magnanimous individual does not confine love to their intimate partnership but spreads it in ripples of goodwill in all directions, honouring the universal kinship of souls. Family and friends have supreme importance, though, for they are most able to give and receive understanding and support.

Nurturing our best and closest relationships is a necessary part of the good life according to hygge. This often will involve getting together in a relaxed, cosy way, perhaps with coffee, cake or beer, and certainly in a spirit of good cheer. The cliché of Nordic angst has no place in hygge: instead we are encouraged to count our blessings, since all we need is available in our immediate environs. Self-denial, too, is regarded as unhealthy, since the finest moments of life are those centred around appreciation, not asceticism. The mindset that vacillates between binging and purging is seriously unbalanced. Instead, the Danish formula for happiness asks us to indulge ourselves with moderation in the innocent side of the sensual spectrum – touch, taste, smell, warmth, comfort.

The friendship charter

Below are some ideas for enhancing the contribution of friendship. Put them into practice, and see whether your contentment is enhanced.

Mix up your friendships rather than keeping friends in sub-sets. Bring friends together and encourage friends of friends to come along. Open-heartedness is key to hygge.

Express warmth to all your friends – by affectionate hugs and by saying how much they mean to you. Break down your natural reserve.

Muster support whenever it is needed. Work with other friends in your circle to ensure anyone in need feels amply supported through a crisis or difficult times.

Get together often – at least monthly. Do not let familiarity deter you – there are always new levels and new enjoyments to explore.

Have regular singsongs, or find some other collective pursuit you enjoy, perhaps dancing, a sport, a board game or a particular kind of outing.

THE NATURAL WAY

TUNING INTO YOUR SURROUNDINGS

Scandinavia offers some memorably dramatic natural spectacles – the lonely waterlogged plains of Danish Jutland, the awe-inspiring fjords and peaks of Norway, the Swedish tundra with its reindeer and lemmings, above all the Northern Lights, that shimmering dance of cosmic energy. However, subtler pleasures, such as the first spring flowers peeping through snow or the kaleidoscopic yellows, browns and reds of an autumn deciduous woodland, also impinge pleasingly on the senses. Such delights can be found even in a suburban garden or city park. Nature spreads its blessings to all of us, if only we can train ourselves to notice them.

"I believe that there is a subtle magnetism in Nature, which, if we unconsciously yield to it, will direct us aright."

Henry David Thoreau

Pleasures of the sky

There is something movingly poignant about the contrast between our loving relationships on Earth and the immensity of the heavens. Perhaps this feeling comes into play traditionally when lovers invoke the moon or the dawn, or wish upon a star. By venturing out at night to view the stars you can enjoy closeness with friends within the grand perspective of the sky, adding a flavour of the sublime to your intimate connections.

The Moon
Choose a full moon and engage in a dance with friends, watching the complex interplay of your dynamic moon shadows in a stately procession of outlines.

Shooting stars
Meteor showers are predictable: they happen when space rocks or meteoroids enter the Earth's atmosphere. Named after the constellation from which the rocks appear to originate, meteor showers such as the Perseids or the Leonids are often so small they burn up in the Earth's atmosphere, leaving momentary light traces – emblematic of life's fleeting pleasures.

Eclipses
An eclipse can be quite scary, since it overturns our preconceptions about the natural order. It is a phenomenon best shared with friends. What better time to enjoy their company than when the sublime unsettlingly and thrillingly manifests itself.

MINDFUL JOY OUTDOORS

Being aware of the nature that surrounds us is part of mindful living. Appreciating its beauty, just as we would appreciate a delicious meal or the warmth of friendship, is in tune with hygge. Indoors we can express our identity with nature by opting for natural objects and surfaces instead of artificial ones, as we have seen (pages 36–41); and we can choose natural materials over synthetic. When the weather is kind, even in winter, we can venture outdoors to expand our horizons and find new phenomena to relish and share. When the weather is *un*kind, we can still go out for a walk, and appreciate home comforts all the more on our return.

Nature in the raw is often aggressive – think of predators such as the owl or wolf, or even robins or kestrels engaged in territorial conflict with each other. However, this is not the aspect upon which we would do well to model ourselves. A better exemplar of behaviour from the natural world would be the opening of a flower or the dissemination of its seeds (indiscriminate generosity), the busyness of bees or ants (productive work) or the protection offered by one member of a flock to another (cooperative vigilance).

"God's gifts put man's best dreams to shame."

Elizabeth Barrett Browning

THE TURNING YEAR

APPRECIATING THE SEASONS

Anyone outside the Tropics experiences seasonal changes over the course of a year – variations of both average temperature and length of daylight. Latitude is key. The closer to the Poles, the greater the trade-off: shorter days in winter, longer in summer. In far northerly or southerly regions, seasonal change is dramatic. The calendar impacts more strongly on people's daily lives, instilling a sense of time's annual rhythm.

The Danish calendar is punctuated by landmark occasions from Christian tradition. Christmas and Easter, in particular, are festivals of communal celebration, each with its distinctive flavour. Whatever your beliefs about God and spirit, participating in the appropriate seasonal ceremonies will connect you rewardingly with your heritage and your community. These occasions are also appropriate times for scriptural storytelling, which perhaps impacts most tellingly on children. Christmas, in any case, is when children glow with excitement, and if you can capture something of this mood, reflected back from their own wonder, it can often be rejuvenating.

ATTUNING TO ANCIENT CYCLES

Since festivals are the perfect pretext for indulging in jolly get-togethers with friends and family, you might consider observing them throughout the year, following the ancient Celtic cycle (see box on page 50). Although this cycle has pagan associations, that does not mean that people of faith have any reason to be wary of it. Its roots lie deep in prehistory. By celebrating these key moments we connect ourselves to the awe and reverence felt by ancient farming communities at the turning of the seasons.

Rejoicing in the Celtic year

This ancient calendar consists of eight festivals: the solstices and equinoxes (quarter days) and the midpoints between them (cross-quarter days). Use these days as pretexts for celebration. Feel free to adopt or adapt traditional rituals, or else devise your own, appropriate to the time of year. (In the southern hemisphere adjustments must be made to the dates to account for the different distribution of the seasons.)

Yule
20–23 December
Winter solstice
(shortest day)
Bring green sprigs into the home; give presents

Samhain
1 November
Festival of darkness
Pay tribute to loved ones lost

Imbolc
2 February
Start of spring
Celebrate new life

Mabon
21–24 September
Autumn equinox; second harvest festival
Give thanks for plenty

Ostara
19–22 March
Spring equinox
Celebrate Easter (when appropriate)

Lammas (Lughnasadh)
1 August
First harvest festival
Celebrate the first fruits of the harvest

Midsummer (Litha)
19–23 June
Summer solstice
(longest day)
Give thanks for light

Beltane
1 May
First day of summer
Dance around the Maypole; crown the Queen of May

FRIENDLY OBSERVATION

The solar calendar, of course, is not merely an aspect of ancient belief and ritual: it is also, more fundamentally, a natural phenomenon that gives rise to seasonal changes in nature. Attuning ourselves to notice and anticipate these transformations enriches our lives by placing them in a larger perspective – the phenomena shared not just by one's neighbourhood or country but by all who inhabit approximately the same latitude. Within the broad framework of change there are moments to treasure. An example would be seeing the first swallow of the year or hearing the first cuckoo. Such moments are personal, but it is good, as always, to share them. Go out with friends to look for the first swallow, rather than relying on chance. You then may have three things to celebrate: the experience itself; the success involved in seeking and finding the experience; and the company of those dear to you.

Some further festivals

The following Germanic festivals may also appeal:

Walpurgisnacht Around 30 April
Night of magic
Light bonfire and dance and sing around it to keep mischief at bay

Yggdrasil Day 22 April
Celebration of the World Tree
Plant trees for future generations

THE LIFE OF THE SENSES

AWAKENING THE WHOLE SELF
Having a healthy relationship with the senses is one of the cornerstones of well-being. Of course, a cerebral person, immersing themselves in books or mathematics or political argument, can find great happiness there. But to close off one avenue just because another one is readily available is flawed as a lifestyle strategy. Such an approach inhibits the development of the whole person. As a general rule, the more we value and nurture sensory experiences, the more rewarding everyday life will become.

A charter for relishing the senses

Here are some suggestions for awakening our senses and learning to come to a more fulfilling and mindful relationship with our physical selves:

- Listen to a storm with others in the dark – or by a crackling fire. Concentrate on the sound of the wind (and the fire) while appreciating human warmth.
- Explore seasonings in your cooking – especially exotic tastes such as wasabi, asafetida and fenugreek seeds or leaves.
- Give and receive a massage – there is no better way to relax and at the same time reaffirm your bond with a friend or partner.
- Take an aromatic bath – surrounding the bath with scented candles adds a luxurious touch.
- Relish luxury fabrics – cashmere and silk, for example, are a special treat for your sense of touch.

EDUCATING THE SENSES

The American short story writer Grace Paley overturned a popular fallacy. 'I don't believe civilization can do a lot more than educate a person's senses.' This idea challenges the myth that education involves shifting our centre of gravity away from the body towards the intellect. In a balanced life we give equal value to all faculties.

The downgrading of the senses, stemming from religious asceticism, has made us less complete as human beings, and in many cases less happy. The truth is that a virtuous life is not incompatible with living fully in the body, alert to the wonderful input from nature and art.

Nowadays our direct contact with reality is under threat from information technology and social media. Society guides us towards data. Instead of appreciating a fine wine without preconceptions we obsess about its provenance and the valuation of reviewers. We forget that our senses can encompass a physical experience more authentically than words can. Hygge entails discovering and celebrating the sensual dimension – including touch, fragrance and taste, all experienced mindfully in the moment.

"Seeing, hearing and feeling are miracles, and each part and tag of me is a miracle."

Walt Whitman

THE JOY OF WALKING

ENJOYING SELF-PROPULSION

Henry Thoreau, the American thinker, used walking as a lens for appreciating his true place in nature. To really become acquainted with a wood, he felt, required a serious commitment to rambling. To canter through woodland on a horse was to miss everything that mattered. To walk, Thoreau believed, was a spiritual activity that helped to bring us in true balance with ourselves and our environment.

THE RHYTHM OF FOOTSTEPS

Scientific research has validated the idea that walking enhances creativity. Traditionally, philosophers walked near their universities to mull over and refine their thinking. There is something satisfying, in any case, about the *pace* of walking. The rhythm of our footfalls seems unambitious, but when walkers look back they are often surprised by how far they have far they have travelled. Travelling on foot gives you time for a truly engaged acquaintance with the landscape, with scope for unexpected encounters *en route*. In fact, much of the most interesting terrain can be accessed *only* by the walker.

In the hygge mindset, walking is satisfying for its back-to-basics character. Leave your cell phone at home or at least cast aside your pace-measuring app: take a refreshing break from technology and participate in a time-honoured activity. What does it matter how many steps you have done? The important thing is the experience itself.

Travelling on foot gives you time for a truly engaged acquaintance with the landscape.

Add a pair of wheels

Cycling, of course, is also self-propulsion, and is popular in Denmark in particular: the country has more than 11,000 km (6,800 miles) of marked cycle routes. The ideal, safest environment is the network of old railway tracks that in many European countries are now cycle-friendly. Part of the pleasure of cycling, as opposed to driving, is that it is eco-responsible, satisfying our deep-seated wish to participate in the stewardship of our planet. If you are shocked by the notion of using a car that weighs more than a ton with the power of 100 horses to transport a person and a briefcase a handful of miles, take to the bike for your daily commute if you can. Hygge means looking after yourself, and the natural extension of this notion is to look after your planet too.

NAVIGATE BY CHANCE

If there are footpaths in your chosen area, use a map and get to know them all – memorize all the options to the point when you can leave the map at home. Go for a walk, either alone or with others, and make your choice of route as you go rather than in advance. When the route diverges, toss a coin or let each friend take turns at deciding on your direction. Such a playful approach adds an extra dimension of interest to the most familiar territory.

TRUTH AND AUTHENTICITY

ENJOYING SELF-PROPULSION
Henry Thoreau, the American thinker, used walking as a lens for appreciating his true place in nature. To really become acquainted with a wood, he felt, required a serious commitment to rambling. To canter through woodland on a horse was to miss everything that mattered. To walk, Thoreau believed, was a spiritual activity that helped to bring us in true balance with ourselves and our environment.

BEING GENUINE
Hygge appreciates the genuine, the authentic, the sincere; conversely, artifice and delusion are potentially corrupting. This scale of values is apparent in the preference for unpretentiousness, and the suspicion of anything like a veneer. The point applies to such aspects of our environment as home décor, but also, more profoundly, to the way we present ourselves to others. Relationships are key to hygge, and unless there is sincerity in a relationship the feelings we express are not outpourings of the heart but inventions of the mind: they are, at worst, calculatedly self-serving.

By extension, hygge asks of us a considerable degree of self-knowledge, since we cannot judge our own sincerity without understanding who we truly are. That does not mean that we are instantly freed from the tensions that come from our various roles in life. For example, we might struggle to balance the demands of being both a mother or father on the one hand and a conscientious professional on the other. Hygge does not claim to resolve such issues. What it does do, however, is encourage everyone to enjoy life within the circumstances that promote the strongest sense of self-worth. These circumstances it identifies in terms of homely comfort and cherished companionship. With our loved ones we can relax into being our best and truest selves.

FORGIVE AND ENJOY

Forgiveness and tolerance play a part in this attitude. We cannot be happy if we live under the constant pressure of self-punishment, as many people do. All too often we inhibit our chances of fulfilment by carrying around a burden of regrets – perhaps even for aspects of our lives over which we had no control.

Implied in hygge is the idea of taking a break from self-analysis – of putting your issues on hold and enjoying the moment. Also understood is that our lives have so much we can value. Among these blessings is the knowledge that you have done your best to learn from your mistakes. Nobody is perfect. Everyone would benefit from working harder to correct their imperfections. But such fallibility need not impinge upon your most enjoyable times, in the home or outside, with others or alone.

Declare a secret amnesty

In any gathering of friends or family there may be someone who has disappointed you in some way, or perhaps even done you harm, knowingly or otherwise. Declare a private amnesty to such people and treat them just like the rest. Be generous, thoughtful, sharing. Give them the benefit of any doubt; or even if there *is* no doubt, be magnanimous. This approach offers them a better chance of showing their own best self, which will benefit everyone present, including yourself.

With our loved ones we can relax into being our best and truest selves.

ACCEPTANCE AND STRIVING

Part of being authentic, it could be said, is recognizing the positive aspects of your own circumstances. Imagine someone who lives in the remote countryside, far from the excitements of the city. Their job options at home are limited; so is the scope for forging new friendships. Some in this situation might endure frustration, constantly dreaming of a life beyond their reach. However, a more balanced individual will focus on the attractions of rural life, getting to know nature and sharing the experience happily with friends. 'But I have nothing in common with these people!' the unhappy dreamer might exclaim. The truth is otherwise: he or she has much in common with other locals, including roots in a shared tradition. Hygge encourages people to rejoice in their provenance, in the blessings of the near-at-hand, rather than strive pointlessly for the unattainable.

That does not, however, rule out ambition. By all means take practical steps to realize your most hopeful prospects, while avoiding the pitfall of neglecting the present while striving towards the future. Share your plans with friends, and call upon their support when your plans seem to flounder. If you do achieve your goal, and it involves leaving the area, be sure to have a tremendous farewell party before you go.

> "The privilege of a lifetime is to become who you truly are."
>
> *Carl Jung*

Authenticity checklist

Mindfully assess your own level of authenticity by asking yourself which of the following characteristics you manifest in your everyday life. If you feel unable to tick any particular statement, ask yourself what you can do to be truer to yourself in that respect. However, be sure to forgive yourself for falling short!

- **You try to be truthful**, while protecting others' feelings.

- **You strive towards sincerity** and avoid pretentiousness.

- **You try to match your actions and words** to your deepest beliefs.

- **You have a good understanding** of your own emotional responses.

- **You avoid situations** where it is impossible for you to be truly yourself.

- **You are true to your principles** even when others disagree with you.

- **You have a clear view of who you are**, and are happy with that identity.

MEALS AND CELEBRATIONS

ENJOYING THE *HYGGELIGT* TABLE

The formula for creating a memorable celebratory meal is straightforward: good cooking using authentic ingredients, with no overcomplicated show-off dishes; cheerful camaraderie; an atmosphere of comfort and welcome; and little touches of all kinds to show your appreciation of the folk who have gathered around your table to share this occasion with you.

There is no need, of course, if you live outside Scandinavia, to follow Scandi recipes. However, a symbolic gesture in that direction, such as a cloudberry preserve or a pickled herring starter, can help remind people of the mood you are trying to create.

If meal marks a specific occasion, participants will welcome a touch of ceremony.

Make a celebratory speech

Participants in a celebratory meal will always be glad to hear a short speech – and will be forgiving of less than Ciceronian eloquence. Five minutes is a good maximum to aim for. Avoid embarrassing anyone. Be sure to express warm feelings – affection, gratitude, admiration and the like. Humour is usually an appropriate seasoning. Keep your language sweet and simple. Use notes by all means as an *aide-mémoire*, but not a script, as this would come over as too formal.

The lucky almond

In Denmark on Christmas Eve dessert traditionally consists of a rice pudding with a warm cherry sauce (Risalamande). Inside is a single whole almond, stirred in at the beginning so that nobody knows whose portion contains it. Whichever guest receives the almond is said to be destined for good fortune all the following year. Sometimes he or she is given a small present. Replicate this principle of a hidden ingredient in any celebratory meal. The element of chance brings innocent fun to a gathering. Such moments are often the most memorable and treasured: grace notes of happiness within the circle of human warmth.

RELAXED CONVERSATION

Although it would be impertinent to lay down restrictions on what to talk about over lunch or supper, the ideal guests will be those who understand that heated political or moral debate is best reserved for the bar or café and has no place in home entertainment. The same could be said of gossip, since hygge is about seeing the best in everyone, including those not actually present.

Cooking and sharing are themselves celebratory, if undertaken in the right spirit, but if a meal marks a specific occasion the participants will usually want to introduce a touch of ceremony too. This might be simply a toast – to a person, a group of people, the assembled company, or the year ahead. Traditional festivities related to the religious or farming calendar (see pages 49–51) will prompt their own special observances. For example, on the longest day you might choose to watch the sun go down – or even gather before dawn to see it rise, prior to staging a midsummer breakfast. Speechmaking and/or readings from appropriate literature can all help to reinforce the mood.

Celebrating love

Valentine's Day (14 February) has become, in recent decades, a highly commercialized occasion when the plethora of hearts and cupids may, for some, be decidedly a surfeit. Anyone who would like to put a less jaded spin on this heavily marketed occasion might wish to try celebrating instead, on the following day, the Roman festival of Lupercalia. This rejoiced in health and fertility. Enjoy a healthy meal and give thanks for fertility, if there are children around, or by extension for plenty in general. You can mark this occasion with your partner, but why not instead broaden the scope to include others – after all, your partnership has riches of warmth and joy that generous souls will want to share. It might be fun too to find a playful equivalent to the ancient goat sacrifice associated with this day – for example, you could offer gifts of goat's cheese to all.

> "Love is the only sane and satisfactory answer to the problem of human existence."
>
> *Erich Fromm*

HYGGE IN A NUTSHELL

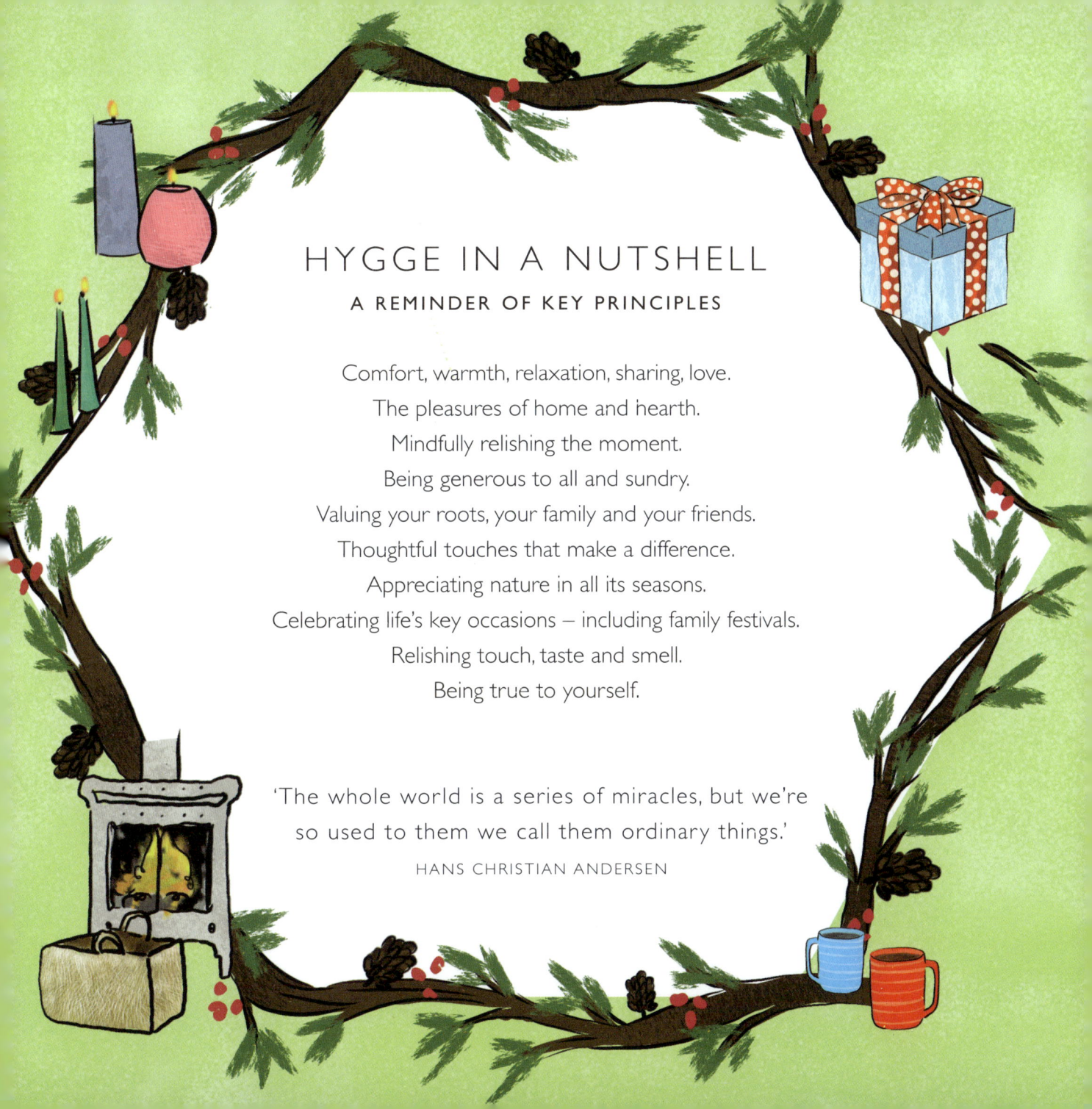

A REMINDER OF KEY PRINCIPLES

Comfort, warmth, relaxation, sharing, love.
The pleasures of home and hearth.
Mindfully relishing the moment.
Being generous to all and sundry.
Valuing your roots, your family and your friends.
Thoughtful touches that make a difference.
Appreciating nature in all its seasons.
Celebrating life's key occasions – including family festivals.
Relishing touch, taste and smell.
Being true to yourself.

'The whole world is a series of miracles, but we're so used to them we call them ordinary things.'

HANS CHRISTIAN ANDERSEN

CHAPTER FOUR

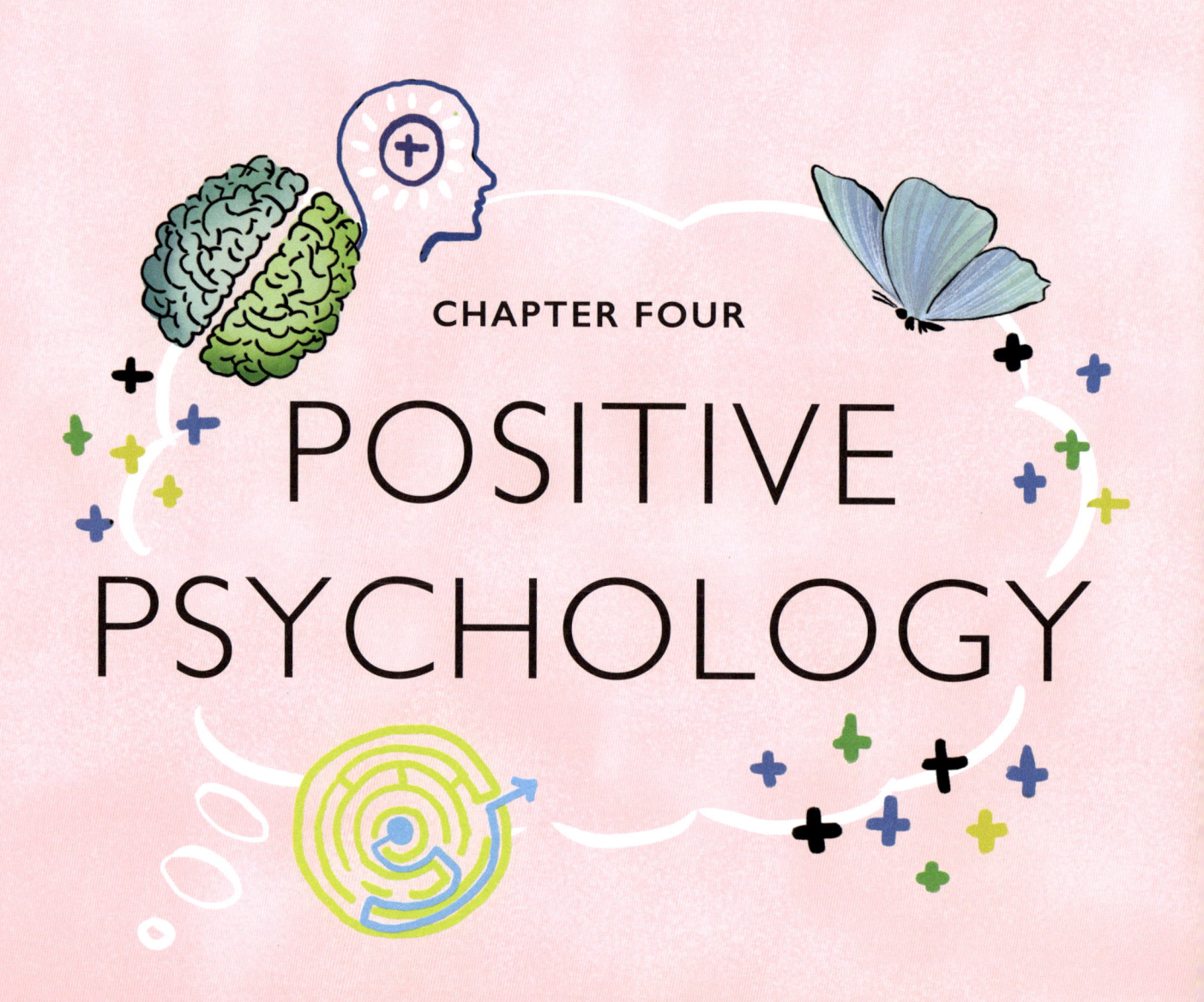

POSITIVE PSYCHOLOGY

How to find happiness by following the key principles of 'positive psychologists', who have taken a scientific, evidence-based approach that emphasizes the value of knowing and using your 'signature strengths'.

THE SCIENCE OF HAPPINESS

FINDING FULFILMENT

Historically, psychology has characteristically focused its attention on mental and social dysfunction, yet one recent branch of the discipline looks by contrast at well-being. This is 'positive psychology', the study of how people can find greater fulfilment in their lives.

It was Abraham Maslow in 1964 who coined the term 'positive psychology', but the main pioneering work came later – from Martin Seligman at the University of Pennsylvania from 1998. Since then writers such as Daniel Goleman, best known for his promotion of emotional intelligence, have helped bring the concept into the mainstream.

Despite its emphasis on the positive, this American-originated school of thought does not imply that regular psychology is flawed, only that the serious mental issues many people face are outside its remit. Instead, it offers the good life as a goal we can all attain by learning a set of life skills. Happiness is not merely the removal of anxiety but a positive mindset we can acquire by nurturing particular attitudes or approaches to life.

Happy nevertheless

In the 1970s Paul Meehl at the University of Minnesota rejected the idea that the human mind is so fragile that it is generally vulnerable to meltdown caused by such negative experiences as criticism, failure or rejection. In fact, many human beings show an extraordinary capacity for resilience, even after enduring trauma. After being knocked down, they come back stronger. The factors that contribute to resilience include, most notably:

- Optimism
- Management of emotions
- Ability to see failure as helpful for learning

EVIDENCE-BASED

Positive psychology is an evidence-based science, which means it has no truck with vaguer concepts of self-help. It starts with an assertion that may be startling to some, although based on extensive research: most people are happy. Moreover, they enjoy a happiness that is self-fulfilling. Their positive mindset results in better enjoyment of study, work, relationships and projects. It may even promote a tendency to better health.

Elements of the good life

Unlike other psychological schools, positive psychology recognizes that the following aspects of life are potentially conducive to well-being:

Happiness This may seem circular, and so it is: happiness is a predisposition, not an outcome.

Flow Finding activities that engage your whole attention in the moment is a mindful process.

The Good Life

Altruism Giving makes you feel better about yourself, and prompts feedback from others that reinforces your well-being.

Talents Knowing what you are good at and exercising that ability appropriately contributes to your sense of purpose, giving your life more meaning.

Virtues Being true to your values increases your sense of self-worth, which enhances your contentment with life.

SIGNATURE STRENGTHS

KNOWING YOUR BEST SELF

According to positive psychologists, the happiest people are those who have found particular strengths and virtues within themselves, and then used them unselfishly. Strengths belong to the realm of character – an example would be empathy or persistence. A virtue involves moral choice: hence, fairness or temperance would qualify. Related to strength is talent, which may require experiment before it is revealed: you cannot tell if you have the makings of an inventor until you try it.

Old schools of psychology often interpreted strengths or virtues as compensations for some negative experience of the psyche, sometimes buried as a memory in the unconscious. For example, someone who becomes a global entrepreneur might, at some deeper level, be compensating for an overbearing father by unconsciously setting out to rival him. Positive psychology sees our strivings in a more positive light. According to Martin Seligman, 'there is not a shred of evidence that strength or virtues are derived from negative motivation.'

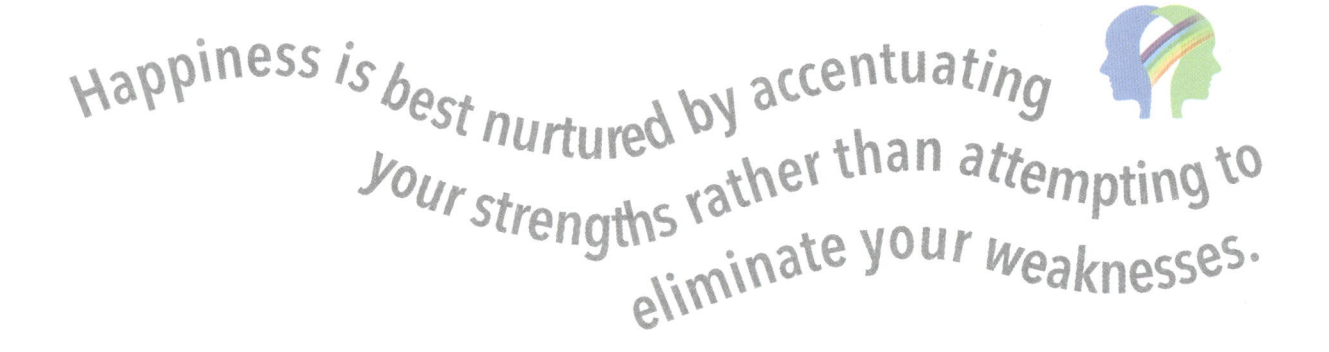

Happiness is best nurtured by accentuating your strengths rather than attempting to eliminate your weaknesses.

POSITIVE PILLARS

Research has shown that accentuating your strengths has a better impact on life satisfaction than attempting to eliminate your weaknesses. Certain character traits such as hope, enthusiasm, curiosity and gratitude have been particularly associated with well-being. Add learned or innate skills to those aspects of temperament and you have a promising formula: a person who does what they are best at in a frame of mind ideally suited to good outcomes. A further dimension is altruism, which acts like karma in rewarding good people by heightening self-respect.

Seligman pointed out the value of finding new outlets for one's signature strengths, rather than being content with habitual ways of expressing them. This gives us a sense of personal growth, of expanding the empire of our self-worth.

Self-assessment

Martin Seligman identified 24 signature strengths, from Creativity and Curiosity to Humour and Spirituality. Here is a simpler classification, subdivided into three groups. On a scale of 1 to 10, mindfully ask yourself for which ones you would give yourself a score of 7 or more. Then for each of these strengths, note the particular activities or relationships where you apply it most effectively. Then see if you can add two further activities or relationships to each list, and take steps as soon as you can to extend yourself in this way in your regular transactions.

Cardinal virtues
These are the four virtues celebrated in antiquity.
Prudence, Courage, Fairness, Temperance

Other moral qualities
These further strengths also have an ancient lineage.
Humility, Kindness, Authenticity, Forgiveness

Executive strengths
These miscellaneous attributes are applicable in a whole range of situations.
Persistence, Enthusiasm, Flexibility, Creativity, Leadership, Judgement

POSITIVE LENSES

LIVING OPTIMISTICALLY

Those who are blessed with optimism tend to be, on the whole, healthier as well as happier – for example, they may have increased life expectancy and better recovery rates from heart operations. Perhaps such outcomes result from optimistic people looking after themselves more. The picture is not wholly straightforward, because optimists can sometimes underestimate risk, and fail to take precautions. What is clear, however, is that optimists are more resilient when misfortune strikes.

To be optimistic is to be confident in your ability to respond well to a challenge. Issues that many would find daunting are instead often seen by an optimist as temporary and manageable. Such a person is good too at compartmentalizing – seeing the true scope of a difficulty rather than enlarging its scale in their imagination. A common variation of this last foible is catastrophizing: lumping together simultaneous issues into one big problem.

THE VIEW FROM WITHIN

Psychologists talk about 'explanatory styles', referring to different ways of explaining the same events. Imagine two friends applying for a job; both get rejected after one interview. One thinks, 'That was bad, I won't get a job, I'm useless.' The other thinks, 'That was helpful, the interview was informative, I can do better next time.' The pessimist internalizes the setback, attributing it to personal failings; the optimist takes a less pervasive view, seeing the event as a learning opportunity. It is not difficult to guess which of the two candidates is happier.

How can optimism be learned? Since optimists tend to invest energy in goal-setting and perseverance, you might think that consciously adopting these approaches would be an excellent starting-point. Good outcomes, however, would be needed to build confidence. A better strategy is to work on your inner processing, as described in the box opposite.

Learning to be optimistic

Learned optimism requires honest self-analysis, and a willingness to probe the roots of a negative mindset.

Half empty or half full?

Take two or three examples of recent outcomes in your life that you believe justify your pessimism.

Mindfully examine each initial situation, the response you took, and the consequences. Ask yourself whether any aspect of your mindset might have made the outcome worse.

Look again at the outcomes, and ask yourself whether your lack of optimism has given them an unfairly negative cast. Perhaps there is a more positive way of seeing each outcome?

Delve into your past and see if you can remember events that might have prevented you from becoming optimistic. Habitual patterns of response can be unlearned. You need to build mindfully on the capacity for change we all possess.

> "A pessimist sees the difficulty in every opportunity; an optimist sees the opportunity in every difficulty."
>
> *Winston Churchill*

GRATITUDE

SMILING FROM THE HEART

Gratitude has the effect of extending a pleasure, in an afterglow of thankfulness. But it is also a kind of gift, in appreciation of what you receive. This allies it to kindness, which is the gift of an empathic gesture.

Benefits of gratitude

It is unclear whether grateful people are happier or whether happy people are more grateful. Positive psychologists have further research to do, in controlled experiments, before this conundrum can be fully resolved. However, the following benefits of gratitude have already been demonstrated convincingly:

- You see people as more generous, more thoughtful.

- You see the world's beauty and wonder as priceless gifts.

- You feel higher levels of well-being.

- You feel lower levels of stress and anxiety.

- You feel closer to benefactors – more affectionate, more trusting.

- You feel more optimistic about life in general.

- You experience a greater sense of belonging.

PRESENT JOY

The importance of gratitude can be seen when we contrast it with regret and nostalgia, which in some ways are its opposite. Regret seeks to reverse time so you can make a better choice. Nostalgia seeks to reverse time so you can enjoy the same choice again. Gratitude is being happy with things as they are or were. It is a deep love of what has happened, and therefore profoundly positive.

Research by positive psychologists has demonstrated what intuition tells us anyway: feelings of gratitude tend to be accompanied by a decrease in negative emotions such as hopelessness and lethargy and an increase in positive emotions such as enthusiasm, vitality and alertness. It has also been shown that the mere act of giving thanks can raise your level of well-being. This effect is easy enough to try, provided you can overcome possible feelings of embarrassment or self-consciousness. The most obvious debt we have is to our parents. Why not tell them how thankful you are for everything they have done for you? You could thank the best and wisest of your old teachers too, if you are still in touch; or a special friend who is always there for you. Many people imagine their gratitude is somehow divined by others, through subtle signals they send out. However, being explicit about your gratitude pre-empts the possibility that your signals are too subtle to be noticed. In any case, hearing words of gratitude is heartening: the pleasure you give will be obvious.

"Who does not thank for little will not thank for much."

Estonian proverb

THE PATH OF KINDNESS

GIVING FROM THE HEART
Caring for the well-being of others increases your own level of well-being. There are three main entry routes to this virtuous circle – *ad hoc* or regular acts of kindness, volunteering, and participating in the life of the community. The benefits in terms of happiness, according to positive psychologists' findings, seem to be especially marked in older people – perhaps because the young often act altruistically under direction from their elders (especially in schools) rather than from personal choice.

ACTING ON IMPULSE
A sense of duty, of serving the society you belong to, is an important motivating factor. This is the moral dimension. However, kindness is most beneficial to the giver when prompted by an impulse of the heart. The starting point is empathy and compassion – kindness being the executive arm of these qualities.

Sonja Lyubomirsky, Professor of Psychology at the University of California, Riverside, discovered that people who performed five random acts of kindness (ideally in a day) reported increased levels of positive emotion. It is easy, of course, to test this informally for yourself. Possible examples might include feeding a stranger's parking meter, writing a letter of support or taking a gift to your yoga teacher the next time you have a class. Good feelings should grow proportionate to the effort you put in. 'Be kind whenever possible,' said HH the 14th Dalai Lama. 'It is always possible.'

Kindness is most beneficial to the giver when prompted by an impulse of the heart.

A kindness manifesto

With a little imagination you could easily extend this programme for living more kindly. Use it as a baseline for further giving.

Tip generously in restaurants and other places when you particularly value the service or feel the person might welcome the money.

Call a friend in difficulty and ask how they are – without talking about yourself at all!.

Do something kind for a neighbour – anything from a lift in your car to doing some gardening for an elderly couple.

Visit the lonely – the gift of your company would be precious to many who are solitary by chance, not by choice.

Take the trouble – for example, if someone asks you for navigational help, take time over the directions and maybe draw them a sketch map. Go over everything twice.

Give thoughtfully – give presents for no reason, and choose something that really shows an understanding of what the recipient needs.

Be anonymous sometimes in your giving – try to perform an anonymous act of kindness every day.

Donate to those in need – for example, in response to public appeals after a natural disaster.

TOTAL IMMERSION

FINDING 'FLOW'

Anyone actively engaged in an activity they find challenging but rewarding, that calls upon their skill set, may from time to time experience a state known as 'flow'. This is also described as being 'in the zone'.

The experience is like nothing else. So much of your attention is given to the task in hand, you cease to be aware of time passing. You know you have entered the flow state only afterwards, looking back. During the activity itself you have no spare attention for self-assessment: you are too busy 'doing'. Artists, in any medium, know flow once inspiration strikes. But you can enter flow while gardening, or playing chess, or dressmaking, or drawing up a five-year plan.

Interestingly, the flow state has no space for emotion, except retrospectively, when you may feel exhilarated. One of its components is being in control. Alongside this, you receive immediate feedback of some kind: you try different approaches and instantly know whether they are working. Above all, there must be an element of challenge, but not so much that your way forward is blocked.

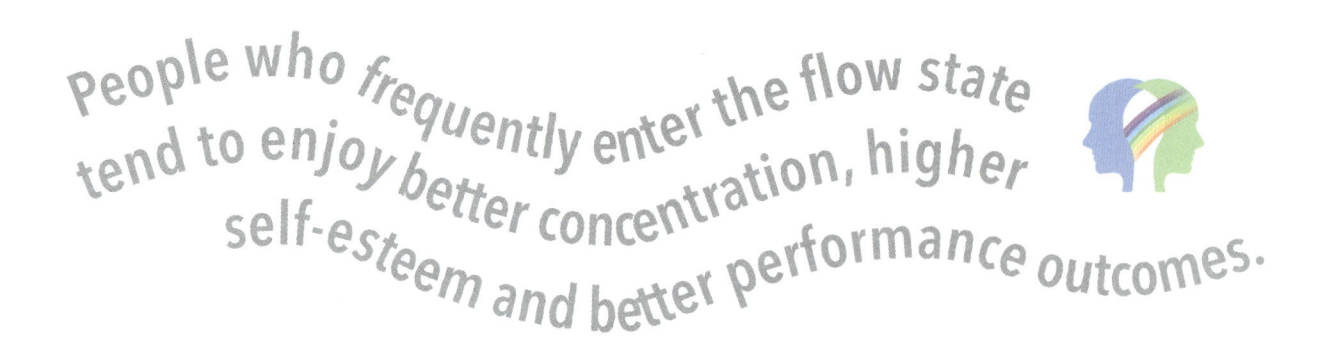

People who frequently enter the flow state tend to enjoy better concentration, higher self-esteem and better performance outcomes.

FLOW AND HAPPINESS

A growing body of evidence suggests that flow is associated with happiness. Moreover, research has shown that people who frequently enter the flow state tend to enjoy better concentration, higher self-esteem and better performance outcomes.

The Hungarian-American psychologist Mihaly Csikszentmihalyi, a pioneer of positive psychology, discovered in the mid-1970s that for creative people the act of creation at times appears more important than the finished work. His studies on flow did much to increase our understanding. In particular, he studied the way many teenagers often choose 'low-flow' activities, such as watching TV, rather than 'high-flow' ones, such as hobbies or sport, despite the greater satisfaction derived from the latter and their long-term benefits. The barrier, arguably, is the effort required for initial engagement: the psychological cost of entry.

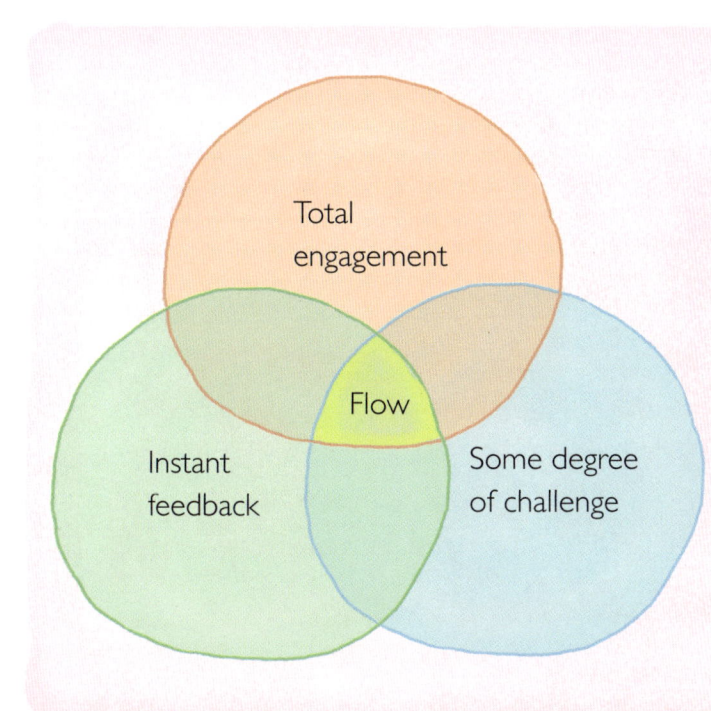

[Venn diagram: Total engagement, Instant feedback, Some degree of challenge — intersecting at Flow]

The Dao: ancient flow philosophy

There are similarities between flow and the ancient philosophy of Daoism, which espouses *wu wei* (non-action) and following the Way (Dao) – that is, using your natural gifts to work harmoniously within your environment. Daoists do not resist their natural tendencies, they surrender to them. They identify with what they are doing. This is a key idea. To identify with your actions is to be totally at one with your experience and your world.

THE ART OF CONNECTION

NOURISHING YOUR FRIENDSHIPS

Positive psychology confirms what you may know from experience: sharing your feelings with others and communicating sincerely contribute to happiness; and having one or more close friendships seems to be one of the open sesames of a satisfied life. Self-disclosure, or unburdening yourself of your emotions, helps to protect people against stress and depression. Moreover, what psychologists term 'active-constructive responding' – listening attentively and offering encouraging responses – can make relationships more fulfilling.

When it comes to friendship, quality seems more important than quantity. You can have many friends and still feel lonely if you cannot share your deepest feelings with them. Students in particular, even gregarious ones, can suffer from loneliness when their conversation revolves largely around academic topics, politics, or impersonal subjects such as music or sport.

TIES THAT FREE

True friends are aware of each other's changing situations, celebrate each other's successes and sacrifice their own time to give care and support whenever necessary. They also channel their signature strengths in the service of friendship, whenever appropriate. There may be times spent apart, but the feeling of closeness returns immediately upon reunion. Having a network of such connections envelops us in love, which is profoundly enriching. For many people, happiness can scarcely be imagined without something approximating to this feeling.

Any experience of exclusion or isolation tends to rob us of our sense of meaning, undermining well-being and bringing a risk of depression. The question arises, how do social media fit into this picture? It has been argued that social bonds are in fact becoming weaker, no matter how many Facebook friends you can boast. The digital interface is not as fulfilling as actual contact. Committing to friendship in actual rather than virtual encounters is a step towards richer living.

Friendship styles

The Greek philosopher Aristotle identified different types of friendship: for mutual usefulness, for mutual goodwill and for mutual altruism. Similarly, positive psychology recognizes four modes:

Acquaintance – superficial, neutral interactions, even if frequent.

Casual friendship – some sharing of thoughts and feelings but little sharing of emotions; not very self-revealing.

Activity friendship – revolving around shared endeavour, based on cooperation; can easily shade into true friendship.

True friendship – authentic emotions shared without anxiety; based on selflessness, trust, empathy and unwavering support.

If you seek more true friendships than you currently have, consider whether you can:

- take any activity friendships to the next stage.

- explore interests you might have in common with casual friends.

- spend more time with certain acquaintances and see if friendships evolve.

- seek friends through an activity circle of some kind – such as a sports club, gym or reading group.

THE PATH OF LOVE

NOURISHING THE CLOSEST BOND

Love is one of the 24 key character strengths listed by positive psychologist Martin Seligman. Mature love between two people creates a context in which both the couple, and anyone dependent on them, can grow and develop — even though there may be times of difficulty. When two partners find mutual encouragement, this nourishes both the relationship itself and the self-esteem of both parties. Mutual trust and commitment also engender positive values such as forgiveness, gratitude and authenticity — being fully yourself within the framework of your partnership. In short, love creates a space where goodness — and happiness — can flourish.

Conflict, when it does occur, is often seen by positive psychologists as something that can strengthen a relationship when there is a real wish on both sides to heal the wounds. If betrayal is involved, this need not be terminal if repentence is genuine and forgiveness lovingly extended. In any case, working at a relationship to realize its full potential is always preferable to simply drifting along together haphazardly. The 'work' should be joyful rather than laborious — if it is not, perhaps your anxieties are sabotaging your well-intentioned efforts?

> "Your task is not to seek out love, but merely to seek and find all the barriers within yourself that you have built against it."
>
> *Rumi*

CONTENTED SHARING

Some psychologists have focused on the value of sharing in a relationship – especially shared projects and leisure pursuits. Equally important are the positive emotions that can be fostered within love, including joy, gratitude, peace and contentment. When contented togetherness is allied to a pleasurable activity, the experience is treasured and memorable, and a succession of such experiences makes a large contribution to life satisfaction.

Relationship action points

Following these suggestions mindfully will help you keep an intimate bond on course.

Embrace change
In a healthy relationship, both partners change, harmoniously with each other. It is unhealthy to want to put a brake on mutual evolution.

Share emotions
Make empathy your watchword. When listening, do not respond to your partner's account of their feelings with an injection of cold reason. Explore emotions together.

Be different
Authenticity is more important than following a boilerplate pattern of how a relationship ought to be. Put your preconceptions aside and be unafraid to be different together. Unconventional relationships can work brilliantly.

Try something new
Exploring new experiences – a leisure interest, a project, a holiday destination – is doubly rewarding when you do it as a couple. Make plans together and pool your feedback. Talk about how you can make it better next time.

THE SCIENCE OF SELF-CARE

LOOKING AFTER YOURSELF
Many people know from experience – their own or others' – that being fully fit, able-bodied and healthy is not a pre-requisite for happiness. In contrast, happiness can be undermined by some ailments that limit your freedom and fill your mind with anxiety. Human beings are resilient and resourceful, however, and many can live happily within the limitations imposed by, say, immobility, or medication's side-effects, or even the onset of serious illness.

Despite this, self-care is an important component of life satisfaction. If you exercise, eat healthily, and get plenty of sleep and sunlight, your mental well-being is likely to be higher. Unhealthy eating and weight gain, conversely, tend to result from low levels of self-respect, often linked with anxieties. To live happily is to appreciate what you have – which includes the body, with all the functions of which it is capable.

EXERCISE AND NUTRITION
Research into exercise has often reported its positive effect on mood – it has even been seen as a possible buffer against depression. Physical activity releases 'feel-good' endorphins in the brain. Some experts point out that exercise distracts us from negative thinking, and perhaps there is long-term benefit from that. There is often an element of personal achievement too: knowing our runs are getting easier gives a pleasing sense of self-mastery.

Nutrition is a complex area, where experts disagree. However, navigating the information labyrinth and opting for eating habits you know to be healthy helps reinforce a positive self-image, which in turn promotes happiness. Snack healthily on nuts, seeds and fruits if you have to – a snack often satisfies an urge for sensation rather than true hunger. Avoid simple (added) sugars, as they release high levels of insulin, increasing both hunger and fat storage. Controlling your diet for health reasons gives extra purpose to your life; if, additionally, your motive is moral (as with many vegans and vegetarians) this purpose has an enriching social dimension.

The sleep of the blessed

Better sleep can improve memory, cognitive ability and judgment. Follow these basic principles to give yourself the best chance of daytime well-being thanks to a sound night's sleep.

Develop a sleep routine – go to bed at the same time each night, and follow the same preliminaries. Habit is relaxing.

Avoid caffeine, vigorous exercise or looking at a computer or TV screen in the hour before bedtime.

If you read in bed, choose something with a suitably relaxed tone – nothing intellectually demanding or action-packed.

Hug your partner, if you are not sleeping alone, and say nice things to him or her. Sleep plus loving contact is a winning formula.

> "Keeping your body healthy is an expression of gratitude to the whole cosmos."
>
> *Thich Nhat Hanh*

FAITH AND PRACTICE

LIVING MORE DEEPLY
Believing in something beyond yourself, and committing to any ritual practices involved, offers orienting purpose and perspective, and sometimes a community of like-minded souls. Fellow-believers often provide a well-organized support network, which helps explain the links that have been shown between faith and happiness – after all, faith in itself is not necessarily always uplifting, because sometimes it is riddled with doubts, or feelings of unworthiness.

Prayer in crisis can be anguished, but when unemotionally routine it can function like meditation, with proven benefits for well-being. Religious ceremonies too can still the mind. Moreover, many believers trust their God is there for them, giving unrivalled reassurance in periods of trouble or stress.

UNIVERSAL KINSHIP
Scientific study of faith's role in well-being is undeveloped still. It is faced with questions of definition. Many spiritually minded people are not regular worshippers, but still gain support from those with similar beliefs, even when these are vague – for example, a view of spirit as a universal kinship: the cosmos of souls. The mind-body-spirit ethos of modern times has created an elastic credo that often fuses three elements: a protective sympathy with nature; an East-inflected belief in karma, compassion and simple living; and an interest in finding peace and harmony through practices such as yoga and meditation.

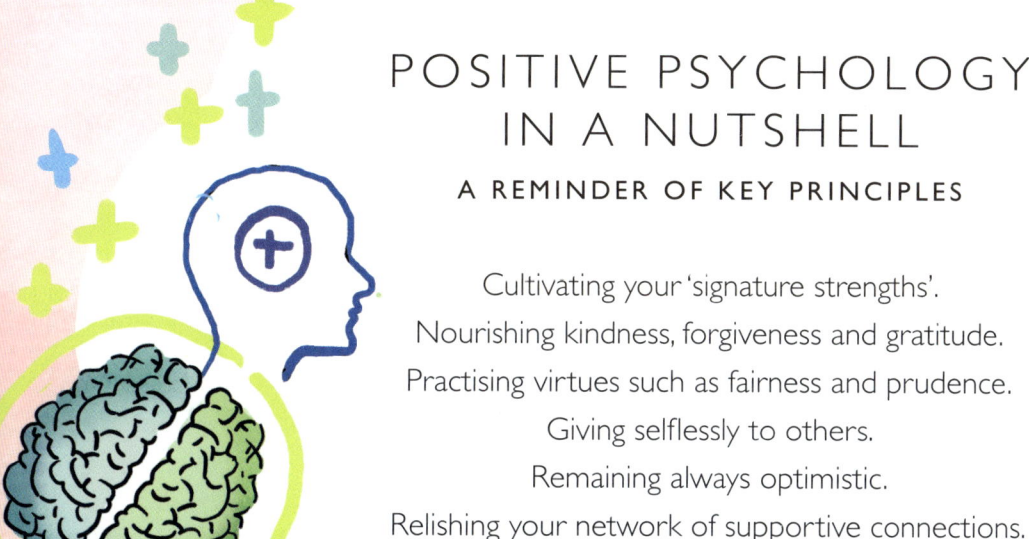

POSITIVE PSYCHOLOGY IN A NUTSHELL
A REMINDER OF KEY PRINCIPLES

Cultivating your 'signature strengths'.
Nourishing kindness, forgiveness and gratitude.
Practising virtues such as fairness and prudence.
Giving selflessly to others.
Remaining always optimistic.
Relishing your network of supportive connections.
Engaging in challenging activities and finding 'flow'.
Developing empathy and compassion.
Maintaining a few true friendships.
Committing to your partnership, if you have one.
Looking after your body, even when unwell.

'The art of living does not consist in preserving and clinging to a particular mode of happiness, but in allowing happiness to change its form without being disappointed by the change; happiness, like a child, must be allowed to grow up.'

CHARLES L. MORGAN

CHAPTER FIVE

LYKKE

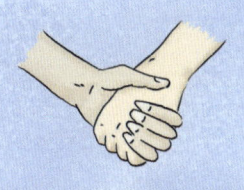

How to find happiness by following Danish research based on the findings of the World Happiness Report, with a particular focus on Trust, Kindness, Forgiveness, Togetherness, Compassion, Possessions and Money.

HOW LYKKE DIFFERS FROM HYGGE

ASPECTS OF LIVING

We have seen (in Chapter Three) how a valued ingredient of fulfilment within the Danish lifestyle is hygge: an emphasis on comfort, generosity, warmth, connection and sincerity. 'Lykke' (pronounced 'loo-kah') is a much broader term, used for convenience rather for any specific set of commonly agreed connotations. It is simply the Danish word for 'happiness'.

In one sense lykke is the brainchild of one person: Meik Wiking, of the Happiness Research Institute in Copenhagen, whose book *The Little Book of Lykke: The Danish Search for the World's Happiest People* is an international bestseller. In another sense the term reflects a team effort to look at happiness levels around the world (as reflected in the World Happiness Report) and analyse the factors in play.

The Report, by experts in economics, psychology and other disciplines, is based on an ambitious world study of self-reported well-being according to a number of wide-ranging surveys, with attention paid also to factors such as mental and physical health, family experience, education, gender, age and the way an individual in any particular country is treated by social structures.

Lykke is an international characterization of what makes our lives happy, based on Danish research.

All this makes the Report sound dry, and indeed it is. However, Meik Wiking's achievement has been to turn the Report's many findings into a set of principles that could be identified as the most reliable ingredients in a happy life, and then weave these points into a highly readable, anecdotally rich account of where people have found happiness not just in Denmark but in every corner of the globe.

Lykke, in short, is not specifically Danish: it is an international characterization of what makes our lives happy, based on Danish research.

This chapter, inspired by Wiking's examination of happiness in six categories (Togetherness, Money, Health, Freedom, Trust and Kindness), explores a variety of ideas and practical suggestions covering approximately the same ground. It amounts to an essay on what really matters.

Our three-dimensional lives

There are aspects of our lives we are powerless to change: our age, our genetic inheritance, our upbringing. Then there is the social and political level which, if we live in a democracy, we can collectively modify, slowly, through our votes. Finally, there is the realm of absolute personal choice. Three-dimensional living involves accepting and coming to terms with whatever we cannot change, and making positive changes where they will benefit ourselves or others. However, bear in mind there is one thing we can always change: the way we respond to situations.

HOW TO LIVE IN TRUST

BELIEVING IN OTHERS
Open-heartedness is usually thought of as a habit of welcome – of making a commitment to give and share without reservation. This is a keynote of generosity. However, that word 'open' can also imply a degree of self-exposure. When we give our trust to others, we do so in the knowledge that we are making ourselves vulnerable – to deceit or betrayal. Yet we continue in our trusting, at least with those chosen individuals we regard as deserving.

Of course, we have all experienced betrayal of trust at some point in our lives. This commonly happens as a trigger to relationship break-up. Many people who have been let down by their partner find it difficult to trust someone new next time around. They evolve towards wariness. They put up defences, and may even steer clear of intimacy for a while. This is understandable, although unfortunate, since one bad apple does not incriminate the whole barrel. Work mindfully to prevent such a response from becoming automatic.

> "Our distrust is very expensive."
>
> *Ralph Waldo Emerson*

Better to commit and be disappointed occasionally than never commit at all.

The question arises: how can we trust others when even apparently trustworthy people so often prove capable of betrayal? A supplementary question is: *why* should we do so?

The why is, to some extent, the key to the how. Mutual trust, quite simply, is the lubricant that enables people to find contentment with each other – whether the context is the family, a group of friends, a neighbourhood, or society as a whole. In offering our trust we are setting personal worth as our default position when it comes to assessing others. To do this is to take an optimistic view of humanity. That does not mean you should leave your home unoccupied without bothering to lock the door: only that in choosing to spend time with the people around whom your life revolves you are making a commitment to believe in their intrinsic worth. You are following a working assumption that they share your core, universal values.

The opposite starting point for assessment would be cynicism: the belief that everyone except you is unreliable until proven otherwise. Love and true friendship cannot flourish under a dark-tinted lens. If everybody mistrusted everybody else, to such a degree, joy would be squeezed out of existence. Better to commit and be disappointed occasionally than never commit at all.

Trust for beginners

Here are three basic guidelines for anyone who finds trusting problematic, perhaps because of previous disappointments. The points here encourage opening up in a controlled way, taking the initiative but without exposing yourself to a high level of risk right from the start.

Offer trust first – in other words, take the lead by committing to anyone who gives you no concrete reason to doubt them. You should, however, start small, offering a minor confidence and then seeing how they respond.

Give people time – do not form instant judgments about people you meet. If in any doubt, give them the benefit of the doubt, and do not hold *everything* back just because you have not yet made up your mind about them.

Do not *overshare* – remember that if you have not yet committed your trust to someone, you can filter what you tell them about your innermost self. Offer small, harmless secrets rather than a major confidence.

A LEAP OF FAITH

One common response after suffering betrayal is to withhold trust with a new person until they earn it. You have been hurt already and are trying your utmost to ensure this experience is not repeated. Unfortunately, though, the guarantee you are looking for will never be forthcoming. Instead, you must have the courage to accept that disappointment is always going to a possible outcome when you give your trust to others, but that happiness will be possible — at least in your close interactions — only if you take the plunge despite this risk.

The implicit undertaking you make when you commit your trust is that you will work through any hurt you endure, and that forgiveness and even reconciliation will be possible at the end of that process. This is just part of life's small print. Totally trustworthy people certainly exist, and may enter your life if you are fortunate, but you will only find such individuals if you surrender your heart to them in advance. Intuition will help you make this less of a gamble: if, deep down, you entertain suspicions you are unwilling to admit to yourself, there may indeed be something wrong. Unless your intuition (not your fear) advises you otherwise, take the risk of trusting.

"**The antidote to fifty enemies is one friend.**"

Aristotle

ACCEPTANCE AND FORGIVENESS

LETTING GO OF HURT

Everyone knows from experience that wishing things were otherwise is a fruitless occupation. A wish has no power to change anything at all, unless wishing is converted to effective action. Sometimes we might wish we had done things differently, but what has already happened is sealed off from our powers of control, immune to change. Regrets cannot reverse the passage of time: all they can do is prompt us, more productively, to resolve to behave differently in future.

Similarly, other people, although we may be able to influence their actions or even their thinking to some extent, cannot be equipped with a completely different set of characteristics just because this would better suit our purposes. If they do not want what we want, we cannot force them into alignment with us: any attempt to change them fundamentally would only end badly.

> "He who cannot forgive breaks the bridge over which he himself must pass."
>
> *George Herbert*

DEALING WITH REJECTION

Acceptance is the process of understanding these basic truths not just intellectually but also emotionally. For example, imagine you have your heart set on a career in the police force and you apply for a traineeship. At the interview you are told, upsettingly (and, it seems to you, arbitrarily), that you are not tall enough to qualify. You know you are powerless to change the rules, and so at the level of conscious thought you accept your disappointment. But does that mean that you can come to terms with rejection emotionally? Not necessarily.

To accept a blow of this kind, or any other kind, you need to reach an emotional acceptance that allows you to detach yourself from what has happened and move on. Mindfulness practice can give you invaluable training in this basic life skill, since it is based on acknowledging our emotions without being drawn into their story. Separating yourself from your inner turmoil allows you to see that it is of no use to you. Instead you can opt for a more positive response. And once you have resolved to do this, and put that resolve into practice, the emotions will fade.

Separating yourself from your inner turmoil allows you to see that it is no use to you.

LET DOWN BY OTHERS

When the source of disappointment is another person – perhaps even someone you like or love – your hurt will tend to be focused not on the event but on the individual who has wronged you. Disappointment can easily turn to anger. Perhaps more than any other emotion, anger is a burden that weighs heavily on the soul, robbing us of contentment. Hence the value of forgiveness – appropriate not because the other person deserves it but in order to still your inner turbulence and find peace. If for any reason you find forgiveness impossible, and you prefer to consign both the offence and the offender to the past, you will still benefit from peacefully letting go of the situation.

If the other person is important in your life, it can help to arrange a conversation to tell them, as unemotionally as possible, how their actions have impacted on you, and to learn about how things were from their point of view.

Forgiveness is valuable not because the other person deserves it, but in order to still your inner turbulence and find peace.

Declare peace

This exercise is designed to help you rid yourself of any resentments and declare an emotional amnesty with those you believe have harmed you. Formally declaring peace in this way can be helpful (even if you cannot find it in your heart to forgive), as it dramatizes your intention to let go of the hurt and makes it more likely you will follow through on that intention.

Set aside quarter of an hour in a quiet place where you feel comfortable. Sit down and relax, eyes closed. Empty your mind. Picture darkness. You are taking time out, in this darkness, from life's rough and tumble.

Summon up in your imagination the person you have negative feelings about. Imagine them in their own home, sitting down similarly and thinking positive thoughts. Resolve that in future you will be able to think about this person without feeling any emotion.

Declare a truce with the situation that has been concerning you. Mentally divest it of its power to make you anxious or annoyed. Speak aloud this affirmation: *'I consign this episode to the past. I am living in the moment in peace, without any burdens from something that no longer harms me.'*

Consider reaching out to the person afterwards in some way if you have decided to forgive them. You are likely to find this a satisfying gesture, freeing your mind of toxins. Normal relations might even be resumed, and in due course you might come to see the problems between you in a different light.

THE JOY OF TOGETHERNESS

NOURISHING CONNECTIONS

Most of us live in continual interaction with others. Much of our pleasure, and much of our pain, happen within this setting. When pain comes from one area of our social or family network there are usually other areas where we can find refuge, solace or compensation.

At times we are alone – ideally as an interlude for recharging our batteries or for enjoying a solo pursuit such as reading, creativity or communing with nature (though all these things can also be done in company). Most of us prefer not to be without the company of friends or family for long periods. However, in later life that can happen. Then, visits from others assume even greater significance, and contact with casual acquaintances can seem like lifelines if you are lonely. Remember this if you encounter such isolated individuals: sharing with them is compassionate and can be rewarding.

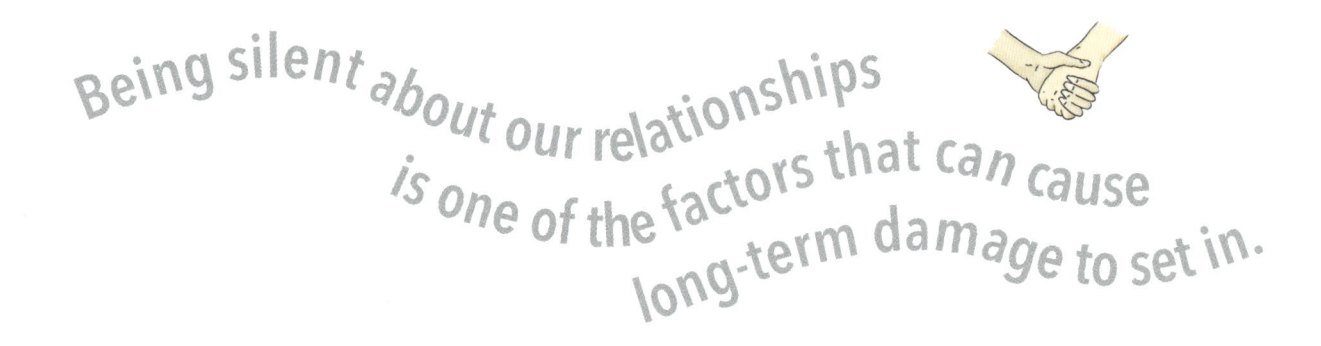

Being silent about our relationships is one of the factors that can cause long-term damage to set in.

Grow and strengthen love

Intimate relationships usually start in mutual attraction but for a lasting bond you need to bring other qualities to bear. Here is a practical game plan for long-term togetherness:

Commit fully

The promise you make to your partner must also be a promise to yourself. If you have reservations, you must deal with them to the point where they no longer arise as issues. Perhaps your partner does not conform to the ideal you were seeking? Then discard that ideal as irrelevant.

Be true to yourself

Deal with your deepest urges, and talk them through with your partner. For example, if you have a yen to travel the world, but then fall in love and decide set up home with someone, admit your wanderlust first. Maybe you can adapt your urges and convert them into something you can share – for example, ambitious annual vacations.

Reaffirm affection

Get into the habit of smiling, hugging, kissing – as gestures of affection or solidarity. Ask about your partner's welfare before sharing your burdens with them. Celebrate your bond by spending quality time alone together when you can. Give without expectation. Create imaginative and pleasurable surprises.

Accept change

If you partner says they would like to make some change in the life you share, do not be dismissive or indignant. Work through the situation together with empathy and flexibility. Possible factors might include the needs of relatives or the demands of a career. Listen with open mind and heart. Experiment together.

LOVED ONES

The phrase 'loved ones' carries a huge weight of meaning. These are the people who are precious. It is important not to take them for granted, as no one is immortal. Also, there is no relationship that cannot be damaged by thoughtless or selfish behaviour. Some relationships turn sour simply because one or other party, or both, fall into habits of neglect – perhaps distracted by other preoccupations. When both sides know a relationship has run its natural course, and both need to move on, no harm is done. Sometimes, however, a failing relationship causes hurt, which may or may not be consciously acknowledged. People on the whole do not speak about their relationships, but silence is one of the factors that can cause long-term damage.

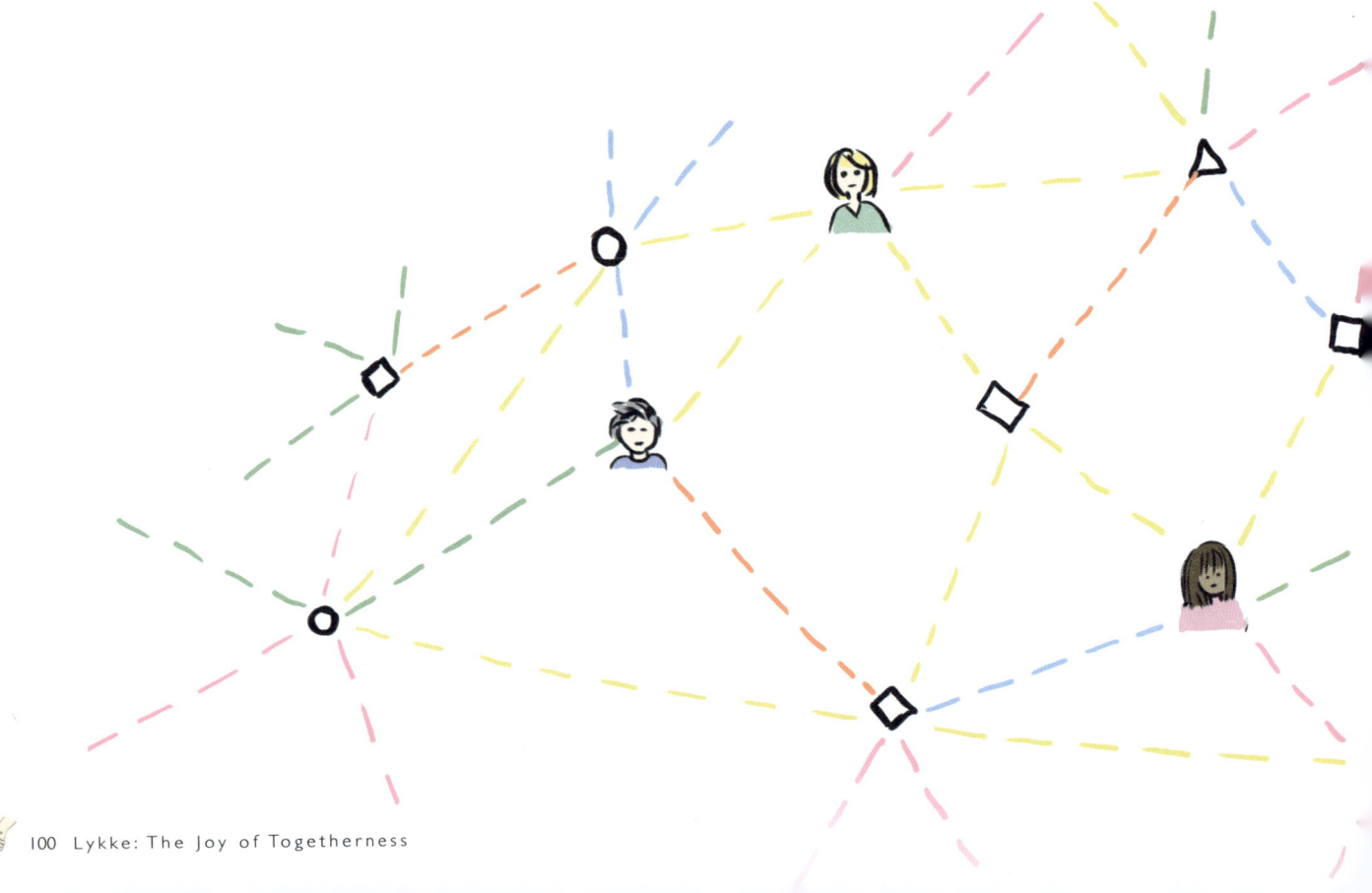

THE WEB OF AFFINITY

To chart any individual's rewarding relationships would be complicated, not least because it would change over time. Often there is an intimate partnership, alongside strong family bonds across the generations. Friendships overlap with this pattern, since we often introduce close friends to our family.

One of the most precious aspects of life is the way that friendships proliferate. Think of how couples become friends with each other: if two friends, for example, both acquire partners, the latter may develop a bond with each other that is closer than the original friendship. Blood kinship remains fixed but friendships criss-cross, constantly evolving.

The web of contact is like a trellis on which a wonderful garden flourishes. Its soil is warmth, openness, compassion, mutual support, cooperation and shared enjoyment of life's pleasures – sharing increases a pleasure, partly because it lays down a memory that either person can evoke for the other. Its sun and rain are the thoughtful attention we give to each relationship, rejoicing in the blessings of togetherness.

Our personal network is complicated further by work, where relationships can flourish as friendships, provided we avoid trespassing into difficult territory. For example, being friendly with a boss can make other employees resentful. Since service with a particular employer tends to be of limited duration, such relationships can often be managed more comfortably once one or other party has moved elsewhere.

FREEDOM AND COMMITMENT

MAKING RESPONSIBLE CHOICES

True happiness, it has been said, has freedom at its core. When you live the life you have chosen for yourself, you inhabit your own vision, rather than following someone else's ideas of how to think and behave. Any norms you follow are obeyed willingly. Peer pressures may exist but if you believe them to be unhealthy, or unsuitable to you in particular, you resist them. Instead, you attend to your own inner voice and respond to its urgings. Happiness, according to this view of life, resides in large part in the choices you make.

TAKING A STAND

There is much to be said for this idea of resisting social pressure when appropriate, though it is far from the whole story. If you belong to a minority unfairly treated within your social context – for example, because of your sexuality, ethnicity or disability – then making a stand may require a great deal of courage. However, the alternatives, which are shrinking into the background or accepting the treatment you are given, may make happiness elusive: just getting by may be a struggle. If you do opt to fly in the face of prejudice, there will no doubt be others who support you. And among such like-minded souls you are likely to find solace, support and even joy.

Freedom taken to extremes can make you an outsider for less creditable reasons. Imagine you believe the tax system in your country is unfair and you decide to participate in the black economy. Not all laws are indefensible but putting yourself outside the tax laws when others who object to the system voice their objections through the ballot box is without doubt morally wrong, quite apart from the harm you could bring upon yourself and your loved ones if caught.

"Life is a classroom, not a prison."

Dr Kathleen A. Hall

FREE SPEECH AND ACTION

In libertarian societies the possibilities for happiness are greatly enlarged, and those who benefit from a benign regime may find it salutary to remember how lucky they are. Taking such freedom for granted is a kind of ethical blindness. It could be argued that those who do enjoy liberty, and other benefits of an open society, have a responsibility to speak out for those who are treated repressively. Certainly, doing so, as with any act of compassion, gives extra value to your life.

BEING RESPONSIBLE

Even in a free society, of course, we acquire responsibilities, which only the selfish try to wriggle out of. This takes us into the realm of ethics and virtue. Most of us feel an inner compulsion to offer help to family and friends when they need it. Looking after ageing family members is often seen as a kind of pay-back for the love and care we received as children, though most people do this as a reflex of the heart, even to the point of heroism. Self-sacrifice of this sort might be stressful in various ways, but that does not mean we would be happier concentrating more on our own interests. Going against the voice of conscience is likely to rob us, ultimately, of our peace of mind. Certain responsibilities simply must be shouldered. Happiness may then lie in the knowledge that we are doing the best for the people we exert ourselves to support.

When you have the life you have chosen for yourself, you inhabit your own vision.

Promise wisely

A promise is a commitment with an implied guarantee attached. That guarantee cannot be enforced, but breaking it tends to damage any relationship based on trust. Often the harm caused by a broken promise could have been avoided right from the start. Here are some guidelines to follow in all circumstances:

Do not promise on behalf of someone else. Phrases like 'I promise you he won't let you down' are intrinsically flawed.

Make an undertaking, not a promise, if you doubt being able to follow through. Phrase the undertaking to match the circumstances – for example, you could set a condition ('provided that…').

Promise your 'best efforts'. This is often the most realistic promise you can make. You could emphasize the extent of your commitment by saying you will do everything within your power to ensure a particular outcome.

Consider what a promise involves whenever you make one. It makes sense to think about the pressures on your time and your capacity for delivering. Are you being too optimistic about the powers you have?

Pull out the stops if you have made a promise that proves hard to fulfil. If the person you made the promise to was hurt or needy, you should do everything you can to avoid letting them down. In any case, you owe it to yourself and them to be true to your word.

EMPATHY AND COMPASSION

LIVING BY THE HEART

We never know how unique our responses are when we intuitively react to a situation. However, most people share a core set of characteristics, some resulting simply from being human, some gender-related, some conditioned by upbringing and social norms. Let us say you received a letter announcing you had failed an important exam. Most of us would probably feel the emotion of disappointment. What would be different from one person to another would be the way that emotion is expressed. One individual might cry; another might swear or screw up their face; another might go quiet, enduring deep feelings while trying to bottle them up.

Empathy is the art of interpreting, from what people do (or do not do) or say, or from the way they look, approximately what their feelings are, and knowing *what it would be like* to be in their shoes.

> "I do not ask the wounded person how he feels, I myself become the wounded person."
>
> *Walt Whitman*

Empathy and mindfulness

Anyone who meditates shows greater activity in a part of the brain called the insula, which plays a part in our empathy for other people. The more you meditate, the greater your capacity for empathy. In mindfulness meditation, in particular, the following process is encouraged. It is as if, in channelling our empathy into a large receptacle inside ourselves, it overflows and spills out for the benefit of other people.

Our awareness enlarges
Initially, in mindfulness practice, we direct our attention compassionately inwards, declining to judge ourselves for any thoughts or emotions we are having.

We attune ourselves to others
This has the effect of enlarging our awareness, and that in turn makes us more responsive to the feelings and needs of our fellow human beings.

We give freely
No longer engaged in pointlessly fighting our demons, we are freed to be more giving. Responding sensitively to others, we give them what we perceive them to need, whenever possible.

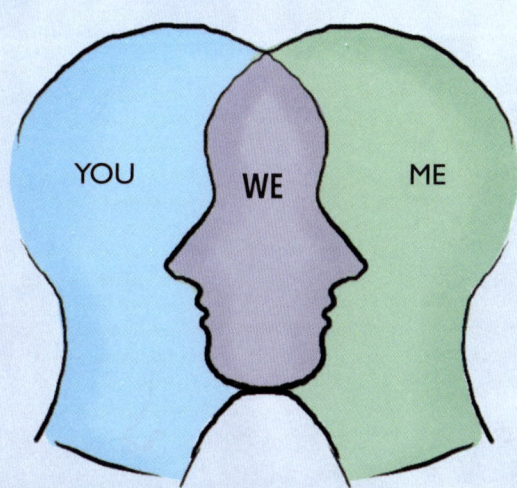

EMPATHY AS A LIFE SKILL

Part of the value of empathy is that it militates against isolation. We can feel an empathic connection with others even when social norms, for example, prevent them from expressing their true feelings. This connection readily becomes a bond of fellowship. Whenever we experience difficulties, we can rely on the fact that they will radiate out to our loved ones (and often beyond), catching their antennae and activating care and concern.

Empathy, moreover, is the gateway to compassion, the portal of understanding that prompts us to act benevolently, not only to people we know but to strangers too. It is empathy that causes some heroic individuals to sacrifice their own comfort or safety for the sake of others – even jumping into a lake to save someone from drowning. More routinely, we apply our imaginations to find practical ways of helping – at least by offering comfort or consolation. Knowing that someone is being empathic towards us – that, in everyday terms, they truly *understand* – goes a long way towards helping us cope with our problems. However, as well as understanding, they might well give us practical assistance too if possible.

Empathy is the gateway to compassion, the portal of understanding that prompts us to act benevolently.

How to nourish empathy

The happiest human beings are naturally empathic: they have an innate ability to understand and share the feelings of others. Ideally we can read subtle signals, such as body language or tone of voice, and imaginatively project themselves into another's place. However, we do differ in our mastery of this basic life skill, and it is always possible to take your empathy to a higher level. Mindfulness practice can help. Here are some further suggestions for deepening your empathy.

Embrace diversity
Try to talk to people from all backgrounds and walks of life, without regard to age or ethnicity. Be curious about others. Do not assume your most valuable encounters will be with your own kind. Invite outsiders into your group. Engage in conversation with the people you meet on your routine neighbourhood errands or while travelling – not just to be polite, but for the sake of what you might learn and find inspiring.

Give help freely
Look for people who can benefit from your help – even if that involves nothing more than listening to them or advising them. Give practical help too when you can. First, assess exactly what help would be most beneficial. Listen to what they say and try to project yourself into their circumstances. Tune compassionately into their wavelength.

Remove your mask
Empathy is a two-way process. As well as attending closely to what someone is saying and/or signalling to you, show your own true, vulnerable self to them, rather than concealing yourself behind a mask. Only then will a channel of honesty and sincerity open up between you.

Stretch yourself
From time to time, do something different. Breaking your routines and venturing into new experiences helps expand your emotional horizons as well as your mental ones. It also brings you into contact with a different range of priorities.

POSSESSIONS IN PERSPECTIVE

FINDING TRUE WEALTH

Some might say we are happy once all our wants are satisfied. But what is a 'want'? If happiness itself is a want, the definition becomes circular. This difficulty is removed if 'want' is interpreted in materialistic terms – a beautiful house and garden, a handsome car, a holiday home on the coast. Yet we all know, since there are parables and real-life stories telling us so, that such manifestations of wealth are too shallow a foundation for a reliable philosophy of life. To rely on material possessions as a basis for happiness is to ground yourself on shifting sands.

What if the stock market crashes and you need to sell everything of value you own? What if your house gets struck by lightning or your holiday home gets flooded? Materialism offers no defence against such misfortunes. In any case, most of us look for a kind of happiness with more depth – one that takes account of love, companionship, laughter, recreation or creativity. The error of materialism is to count the tangible while ignoring the intangible. True, if you have a yacht, you have the potential to enjoy a fabulous sailing holiday. However, why should that be a happier experience than ferry-hopping on public transport?

To place too much faith in material possessions as a basis for happiness is to ground yourself on shifting sands.

QUESTIONING THE HIGH LIFE

The answer to this last question might focus on luxury. The good life, a hedonist might argue, is essentially the high life. In fact, luxury tends to be appreciated as much for its psychological symbolism as for its intrinsic qualities. Often at its core is restful ease: others do the work for you. Rest, however, is available at times to all of us, regardless of wealth or income. So is the beauty of nature. So too is sensory intimacy – the touch of love.

Understanding the superficiality of luxury as an ego-boosting status symbol is different from resisting its lure. Many of us become attached to possessions, often as lifebelts on uncertain seas. You might value the perfection of something newly acquired – and be upset about even a slight mark of damage. Alternatively, you might invest sentimental value in some memento – an heirloom, or jewellery given by a loved one. If you have lost somebody, such an object can seem like a priceless surviving part of them. As with luxury, there is psychological symbolism at work here, but of a more creditable kind.

True belonging

In resisting the lure of possessions, we should not fall into the trap of believing that all attachments are worthless. Here are some guidelines on the kinds of exterior object or phenomenon to which we are entitled to attach value:

Home
The sense of home can be satisfied without possession: not all societies have an owner-occupier tradition. Home is where you feel most grounded, most able to relax and share love. It is natural to want to put your own things in your own home, but bear in mind that something found or given can be just as precious as something you have paid a lot of money for.

Heartland
As the setting for treasured memories, the place where our roots lie looms large in our consciousness. To see such places change under pressure of modernization can be painful. Your memories, however, are inviolate, for as long as you retain your mental faculties.

Souvenirs and memorabilia
A few precious items will normally be enough to evoke past happiness. Some people, however, cannot bear to discard anything that links them with the past. If you fall into this category, some mindful decluttering might be in order. The past can unhealthily crowd out the present if you let it.

Love tokens
Most love tokens, most notably rings, are small enough to accommodate at home without difficulty – but also to be easily lost. It is worth considering having a safe at home where you can store such small symbolic, often valuable items.

TREASURES WITHIN

It is well known that our true wealth lies within. This is only partially true, since other people are such an important component of our inner estate. However, those people are often said to dwell in our hearts and we in theirs.

Definitely within ourselves is the set of values and talents that gives us the potential to be creatively ourselves. This collection of personal qualities is the focus of both Japanese ikigai (see pages 118–139) and the Western concept of positive psychology (see pages 64–85). The search for happiness, according to this view, is the search for our destiny, the attributes we can apply to make the most of our birthright as human beings in our particular time and place.

> "The earth is the general and equal possession of all humanity and therefore cannot be the property of individuals."
>
> *Leo Tolstoy*

MONEY WITHOUT WORRY

BEING CONTENT ON A BUDGET

Money anxieties adhere to a whole range of commonplace situations. Trying to establish or enlarge a family in a home of your own can be economically stressful. At the other end of the timeline is the squeeze in retirement, when you have plenty of time but often not enough savings or pension to make the most of your new-found leisure. In between come various crises and chronic shortages, from boiler breakdown and divorce settlements to unemployment and healthcare costs.

In addition there is the cost of aspiration, of striving to afford symbols of high status: home, garden, car, school and holidays. It seems that money-seeking can become a behavioural addiction, akin to gambling or alcoholism: the brain's chemistry can be changed, producing a 'high' when money rolls in.

Whenever we start to view money, and the high-status lifestyle it unlocks, as important to our self-image, we become vulnerable to what Carl Jung calls the 'shadow' – the dark side of the psyche. This is a miasma of insecurities. Our relationship with money becomes all-consuming, damaging the relationships that are truly valuable – with other people, with our own self. Mindfulness, as so often, can break this stranglehold. Defining and committing to our true values, while recognizing the emotions stirred by money and refusing to let them shape our choices, is the path to a more balanced attitude.

A mindful money meditation

Use the following meditation to readjust your thinking and relegate money to its rightful place as a tool that serves you.

Sit comfortably and clear your mind of thoughts. Breathe deeply and slowly. Fully experience the moment – the sensations you are feeling, including the rise and fall of your own chest as you breathe, and the pressure of the chair.

Notice the absence of money from your present experience. If you take time out from money anxieties, nothing changes: life remains precious and sweet. Think of all the times ahead that will *not* be affected by money issues (some will): your evenings in with your partner, your expeditions into the countryside, your family meals, your lovemaking.

Think of real money, sitting in a bank, and then think of ghost money – the form it takes when it haunts you. You may not be able to solve your money issues immediately but you can refuse to let them take residency in your mental landscape.

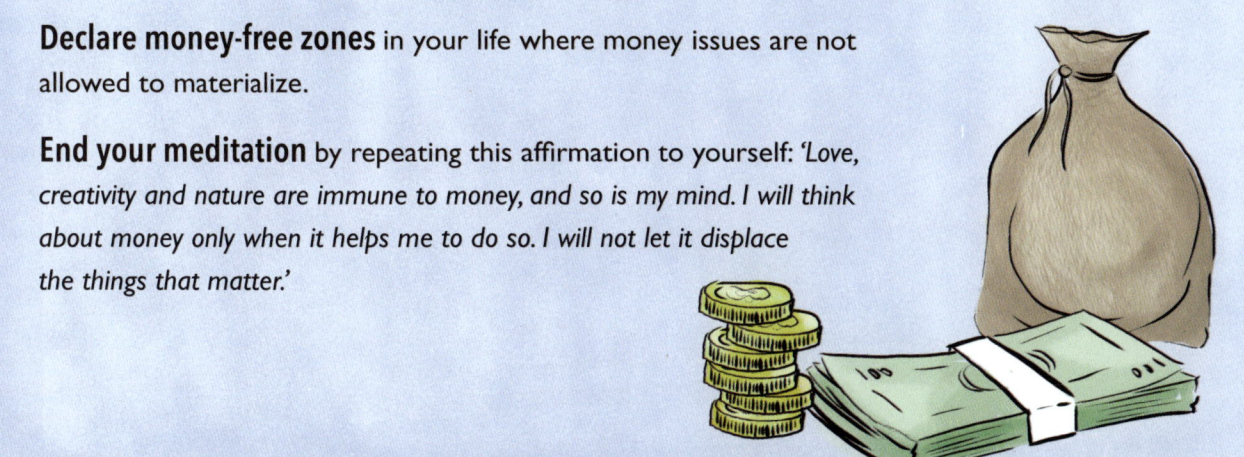

Declare money-free zones in your life where money issues are not allowed to materialize.

End your meditation by repeating this affirmation to yourself: *'Love, creativity and nature are immune to money, and so is my mind. I will think about money only when it helps me to do so. I will not let it displace the things that matter.'*

Lykke: Money without Worry

ENOUGH IS ENOUGH

It is true that not having enough money closes many of life's doors. However, once you have enough to support a comfortable lifestyle, there is no evidence that greater means will make you happier. In modern times, the perceived link between money and contentment is breaking down, under pressure from the mind-body-spirit ethos. Buddhism warns of the dangers of attachment. Many of us opt to downshift, regarding money horizontally, as a tool for transactions, rather than vertically, as a ladder to our dreams.

Affluenza blues

The term 'affluenza', first used in 1954, is a hybrid of 'affluence' and 'influenza'. It describes the contagion of debt, anxiety, overwork, overconsumption and waste that results when a consumerist society binges on acquisitiveness. Wealth inequality increases and happiness levels decline, for both haves and have-nots. British psychologist Oliver James has explored the political roots of affluenza, attributing it to the more selfish varieties of capitalism in English-speaking nations, compared with Europe.

Once you have enough cash to support a comfortable lifestyle, there is no evidence that greater means will make you happier.

LYKKE IN A NUTSHELL
A REMINDER OF KEY PRINCIPLES

Trusting other people.
Bravely committing the heart.
Letting go of hurts caused by others.
Forgiving when you can.
Relishing your web of affinity.
Growing and strengthening love.
Accepting inevitable change.
Making free choices while accepting responsibility.
Developing empathy and compassion.
Keeping possessions and money in perspective.

'The art of living does not consist in preserving and clinging to a particular mode of happiness, but in allowing happiness to change its form without being disappointed by the change; happiness, like a child, must be allowed to grow up.'

CHARLES L. MORGAN

CHAPTER SIX

IKIGAI

How to find happiness by drawing upon the Japanese concept of ikigai – in other words, the sense of purpose that prompts you to get up in the morning with enthusiasm and resolve.

TRUE PURPOSE

FINDING YOUR ROADMAP

According to the Japanese, everyone has their ikigai, though he or she may not be aware of it. The word means 'reason for being'. Although less of a fashionable cultural phenomenon than the Danish hygge, ikigai is more comprehensive and also more demanding, since it involves self-exploration. However, the effort applied soon pays off, delivering to each individual a roadmap for navigating life's countless choices and opportunities.

Ikigai is all about purpose, which we often speak of in terms of gain or loss. To *find* our purpose is a clarifying and reassuring experience: where there was uncertainty there is a now a clear way forward. To *lose* our purpose is disorientating and disabling: we now longer know where to channel our energies.

WAKE-UP CALL

'I need a reason to get out of bed in the morning.' This often-heard expression reflects a psychological truth, which is the connection we feel between our energy levels and our optimism for a good outcome. We face the day more positively when we have a set of goals in prospect as well as the belief that some of those goals – even if only small ones – might well be attained.

Often we will wake up to face a day of challenges. When this happens, having a definite purpose is rather like having access to an inner ally. Having already made the commitment to do the best we can in the light of well-defined priorities helps us get out of bed with optimism. Without this compass bearing we might opt instead to bury ourselves under the covers.

THE FOUR-LEAFED CLOVER

Ideally, we have a *composite* sense of purpose, in which campaigning for a particular cause or pursuing a personal project is balanced against other sources of motivation, both personal and (except for retired people) professional.

Imagine a lucky four-leaved clover as a representation of your composite purpose. The leaves might be taken to symbolize the following dimensions of life, stated here with a typical selection of possible elements:

Possible purpose:
Learning new skills
Succeeding for your company
Gaining promotion
Building an effective team
Finding new employment

Possible purpose:
Starting a family
Healing a breach
Helping someone troubled
Making new friends
Caring for someone

Possible purpose:
Giving charitably
Helping neighbours
Campaigning for change
Smartening up your street
Teaching literacy

Possible purpose:
Losing weight or getting fit
Writing a novel
Running a marathon
Creating a beautiful garden
Learning a language

Ikigai: True Purpose 121

PURPOSEFUL PATHWAYS

CHOOSING YOUR DIRECTION

The words 'goal' and 'purpose' have different connotations. A goal is well-defined. The implicit football metaphor suggests precision: you run around the pitch, dodging and tackling, losing and gaining possession of the ball, but the idea is to kick that ball beneath the crossbar. A goal, once achieved, is a moment of victory, a cause for celebration. If you are following a purpose in life, you may indeed find reasons to celebrate, perhaps often if you are fortunate. However, your joy is most likely to revolve around the attainment of specific goals *within* your purpose.

Purpose is often complex, resisting easy definition – a set of parameters rather than a fixed point you are attempting to reach. If you feel purposeless, perhaps you do have a purpose but one you do not yet recognize? This is a common phenomenon. Finding your purpose more often requires looking inside yourself rather than outside. Or rather, you look inside to find your motivating energy and outside – often in your immediate vicinity – to find your goals and signposts.

Purpose is often complex, resisting easy definition – a set of parameters rather than a fixed point.

Three turns of destiny

If you remain mindfully alert to opportunities that serve your purpose, you may be surprised how often such opportunities become apparent. The strength of your purpose seems to re-orient life around you, like iron filings around a magnet. This phenomenon, of the means readily presenting itself to the purpose, has been dubbed the 'law of attraction'. Here are the stages you need to follow to exploit this effect.

Set your vision
Consider how you see yourself in the future. Your purpose at this point may be general — for example, leading a more gregarious life or moving closer in some way to nature.

Identify goals
It is rewarding to have goals to aim for, but do not pursue too many at once, and be sure they do not conflict with each other. Be open to finding new goals as well as jettisoning unproductive ones.

Look for signposts
Having faith in your purpose will help you recognize signposts when you see them. This is where the law of attraction comes in. Through self-belief you will find your destiny.

Cornerstones of purpose

Although we are all wonderfully different from each other, certain fundamental human needs can be identified. The following graphic shows (with modifications) our psychological needs as defined by Abraham Maslow in 1943. Any can provide a basis for purpose: some of the more obvious possibilities are suggested here. Maslow saw the needs he identified as a progression, with 'self-actualization' at the apex of an imaginary triangle. We move up the triangle as we satisfy our more basic needs, progressing to a higher level of aspiration. However, with regard to purpose, this hierarchical approach is misleadingly oversimplified. For example, if your purpose is to compete in the Invictus Games, this is a fitness vision that also reflects an appetite for self-fulfilment and esteem, while also feeding into connection (fellow feeling with other disabled sports contenders). If your purpose is to create a self-sufficient garden satisfying all your family's vegetable needs, this operates at a basic level (food) but also at the aspirational level (self-fulfilment), as well as being an aspect of family life (love/belonging).

Maslow's psychological needs and related purposes

Self-fulfilment
Self-expression, creative project, rewarding job, lifelong learning, exercising a skill

Esteem
Promotion, prize-winning, exams, qualifications

Love/belonging
Family, partnership, children, friendships, social groups

Health/fitness
Keeping fit, overcoming illness, ageing well, comfortable retirement

GOALS AND SIGNPOSTS

A signpost sets you going in a particular direction – not motivation but routefinder. Imagine you have fallen in love with someone Japanese. You decide you would like to create a home and family together. Your *purpose* might be to overcome the cultural barriers and frequent misunderstandings between you to reach a shared empathy, a closer bond. Within the boundaries of that purpose you choose your *goal*: to learn Japanese, or rather, since goals need to be more specific, to *become fluent* in Japanese. Now, the company you work for imports its products from Japan, and when a new vacancy is advertised in the sales department you apply, having meanwhile started evening classes in beginner's Japanese. The vacancy, and the language course you see advertised in your local library, are signposts. Together they set your direction.

To gain life satisfaction from a purpose, or ikigai, you need to understand its requirements and be alert for opportunities as they arise. Sometimes potentially fruitful chances will present themselves in disguise. The more you apply your imagination, the more likely you are to recognize these hidden pointers. Challenges will also feature as you scan your possible field of action. However, if you have strong purpose you will approach any hurdle with determination.

> "The moment you are old enough to take the wheel, responsibility lies with you."
>
> — *J.K. Rowling*

A LIGHT TOUCH

AVOIDING SINGLE-MINDEDNESS
If ikigai is the journey that gives satisfying shape to your life, this shape is an arc of aspiration within which, paradoxically, we can find peace. Purpose and peace are far from being at odds with each other – unless, that is, we are 'driven'. To be driven is to be so attached to a goal, or set of goals, that the possibility of failure is unthinkable. Driven people push themselves – never a recipe for happiness. Instead of pushing, let your vision lead the way, as you follow it with a light, optimistic step. Great effort may be required of you from time to time, but ideally it will not be anguished: it will be hard work cheerfully undertaken.

STAY IN THE MULTIVERSE
To be single-minded is to channel your energies towards an all-consuming target. However, it is not only your energies that are narrowed in this process: so too are your horizons. Being fixated on one aspect of your life is likely to impact badly on other aspects. In particular, important relationships often suffer when you sacrifice your time to pursuing a single goal.

Imagine you have been slandered. You plough time and money into fighting the case. Maybe you win. But you have also lost, because the case has damaged your relationship by introducing an external obsession into your talk with your partner, even in the bedroom. They have seen a darker side to you.

LEARNING TO FAIL
Another concern about those who follow purpose single-mindedly is that failure is likely to hit them hard. A major advantage of having a composite ikigai is that disappointment in one aspect might be balanced by hopeful progress, or even triumph, in another. In any case, being lightly attached to your goals makes it more likely that you will learn from them when you fail.

> "There is no failure except in no longer trying."
>
> *Elbert Hubbard*

How to deal with failure

Failure, when it happens, is best faced full on. Follow these strategies:

Share your experience A friend or ally can offer invaluable insights. Select someone who will listen and empathize, not to try to solve your problems.

Let time pass There is no need to rush your next move. Take a break and think things through.

Avoid blame Do not present yourself as a victim either. Allow yourself an emotional reaction but try not to enact that response in what you say or do.

Learn from the experience This is the essence of 'failing well'.

Stay resilient Never believe you *are* a failure: this switch from the act to person deserves no place in your mindset.

HOW TO FIND MEANING

MAKING SENSE OF THINGS

Following a purpose gives meaning to our lives as well as direction. It helps us make sense of the here and now.

The old cliché that happiness is a journey, not a destination, helps to explain how this idea of a meaningful life might come about. On account of having a purpose, your life acquires more depth, because the present is placed within the context of two different time zones: the future you travel towards and the past where you have acquired experience you can learn from. Mindfulness emphasizes the present moment. But a present enriched by future goals and past learning goes beyond mindfulness in creating for yourself a fully rounded, meaningful life.

Tripod of purpose

There are three factors that make it likelier you will be able to pursue your *ikigai* more successfully, thereby opening up a world of meaning:

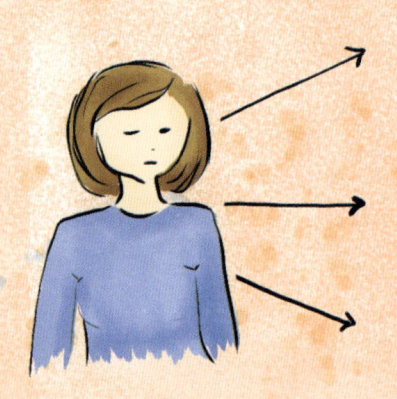

Mental and physical health Being free of health worries give you mental and physical space in which to follow your purpose.

Independence Having the freedom to make choices over your use of *some of* your time and energy, even if the rest is accounted for by binding commitments, is also conducive to purpose.

Connections A network of people who give you practical and emotional support creates a stable platform from which you launch your personal endeavours.

The meaningful life

Past experience enriches through
Wisdom

Present experience enriches through
Purpose

Future vision enriches through
Optimism

WHY AM I HERE?

Directionless people often think of their lives in terms of human existence in general. Does life itself have a purpose? This line of inquiry might take you into philosophy or religion but, either way, a troubling doubt might set in. Both philosophy and religion aim to eliminate doubt, replacing it by certainty (in the one case) and faith (in the other), but neither certainty nor faith comes easily.

When following a purpose you are less likely to find yourself adrift among such massive imponderables. Therefore, in this sense too it could be said that purpose generates meaning. It gives greater significance to the place in life we inhabit.

THE BIGGER PICTURE

A sense of contributing to someone greater than yourself tends to enlarge the amount of meaning attached to an endeavour. This is most obvious when you work for the benefit of others – aiming, for example, to be a good sales executive or to campaign for gender equality or tighter conservation laws. However, when our purpose comes from a creative project, this too we tend to treat as bigger than ourselves – it invests life with an aura of meaning.

PURPOSE FROM WITHIN

IDENTIFYING YOUR TALENTS

It would be wrong to picture ikigai as a harvest equally available to everyone. In truth, we each have an inner grove of ikigai trees, and everyone's grove produces a different variety of fruit.

Often in life it might appear to make sense to go against the grain of your nature. For example, if you are shy, you might choose to attempt to overcome your inhibitions by thrusting yourself into the social whirl. However, if you are also artistically talented, no doubt it would be more rewarding to follow a vision of yourself as a successful artist than as a political leader. You could still work to overcome your shyness while pursuing your creative ambitions. This way your general direction of travel would be *along* the line of your true potential.

The sideways move

Like the knight in a chess game, it sometimes makes sense to move sideways, to a position where you can more readily exercise your special talent. A classic example would be in employment. Imagine you are a graphic designer who for years has drawn historic architectural features as a hobby, and in the process learned much about the subject. You show your drawings to a firm of architects specializing in conservation, and ask if there might be an opening for you. Thereupon they recruit you on trial to join a team surveying an important historic building. Mindfully be on the alert for such sideways opportunities. Who said a personal pathway has to be linear?

STYLES OF EXCELLENCE

Doing what you are good at can be a quick route to fulfilment. Struggling against the grain of your own nature to overcome a deficiency tends to be slower and less likely to be productive. Bringing excellence into the world usually involves people identifying their innate talents and then finding a suitable stage on which to express them.

We often waste time worrying about our failings while ignoring a more rewarding focus for our energies: our existing skill set. Recognizing our skills often requires us to go beyond the limits of our publicly recognized achievements and formal qualifications. There are whole areas of personal expertise that tend to be undervalued – for example, in the educational system and in the workplace. You might be a brilliant persuader or mediator, or a meticulous observer with a sharp eye for detail, or an exceptional 'people person'. If you possess a special talent – and we all have one – you will eventually find the appropriate arena for action and success provided you recognize your ability and apply your imagination to find its appropriate outlet.

We each have an inner grove of ikigai trees, and everyone's grove produces a different variety of fruit.

HAPPY JOURNEYS

TAKING PLEASURE FROM A QUEST

Often we sacrifice our comfort and convenience for the sake of the vision we pursue. Think of students, burdening themselves with debt and accepting, in many cases, a frugal lifestyle. They may not even be motivated by dreams of future prosperity but instead by passionate commitment to the subject, and also perhaps by the collegiate life, with its scope for deep friendships seasoned by intellectual debate.

This is not a case of sacrificing happiness now for the sake of future happiness. Even though students are increasingly beset by mental health issues, many are happy in this transitional phase. There is no reason why this pattern should not also be widely found in adulthood: the acceptance of material limitation (for example, debt or parsimony) for the sake of a richly satisfying endeavour. Having found a purpose, we may find it enriching even before any goals have been attained. A vision revolving around some kind of training fits this category ideally, which is why the concept of lifelong learning is so appealing.

SOMETHING SPECIAL

Choosing a purpose need not be a question of looking at all available options, as if advertised in a catalogue. Many people create their own unique purpose, which comes out of their values and interests. For example, someone committed to the belief that children produce exceptional art, because they have not yet learned to be inhibited, might just conceivably be inspired to start a gallery of children's art in a fashionable art district of a city, scouring the country's schools for the most talented young artists and channelling the sale proceeds into charity. This is a fictional example, but plausible. A unique purpose is uniquely satisfying.

Sharing the path

Although the student environment is uniquely gregarious, in adult life our ikigai may be solitary, even when learning is part of it. However, since much of our happiness comes from our connections, sharing your path is likely to make it more rewarding. The following approaches might help to introduce an element of sharing into your enterprise:

- Persuade a friend to join you in your purpose, travelling with you at least some of the way.
- Use social media to find like-minded souls on a similar journey – people you can swap experiences with.
- Join – or start – a regular group for those taking your path. Go to meetings and invest energy into appropriate initiatives. Find people on the same wavelength.

MINDFUL MOMENTS

APPRECIATING INCIDENTALS

As we move forwards on different fronts, it is good at the same time to look around us. Ken Mogi, author of *The Little Book of Ikigai*, identifies two of his Five Pillars of ikigai as the 'joy of little things' and 'being in the here and now'. These phrases point to mindfulness, the practice of being fully aware in the moment (see pages 28–31 and 178–181). Being attentive to your surroundings, to everything that happens within the scope of your perceptions, provides purpose in your life within an enriching context.

Of course, mindfulness can serve your purpose directly, as a tool for heightened awareness – an invaluable ingredient in assessing your talents, identifying your goals and knowing what needs to be done, with what resources and with what likelihood of success. However, mindfulness is all-embracing: a principle to live by rather than an instrument only for specific tasks. If you treat your whole life mindfully, attentive to all aspects of experience, you will find ikigai takes its proper place within a life fully lived.

A simple analogy makes the point. If your purpose is a path, and you are intent on moving along it, you will scarcely bother to look at your feet. However, if you did, you might see a profusion of inconspicuous, beautiful wild flowers. They are totally unconnected with your purpose. But unless you leave space in your life for the incidental, you will miss much of value.

The mindfulness/purpose balance

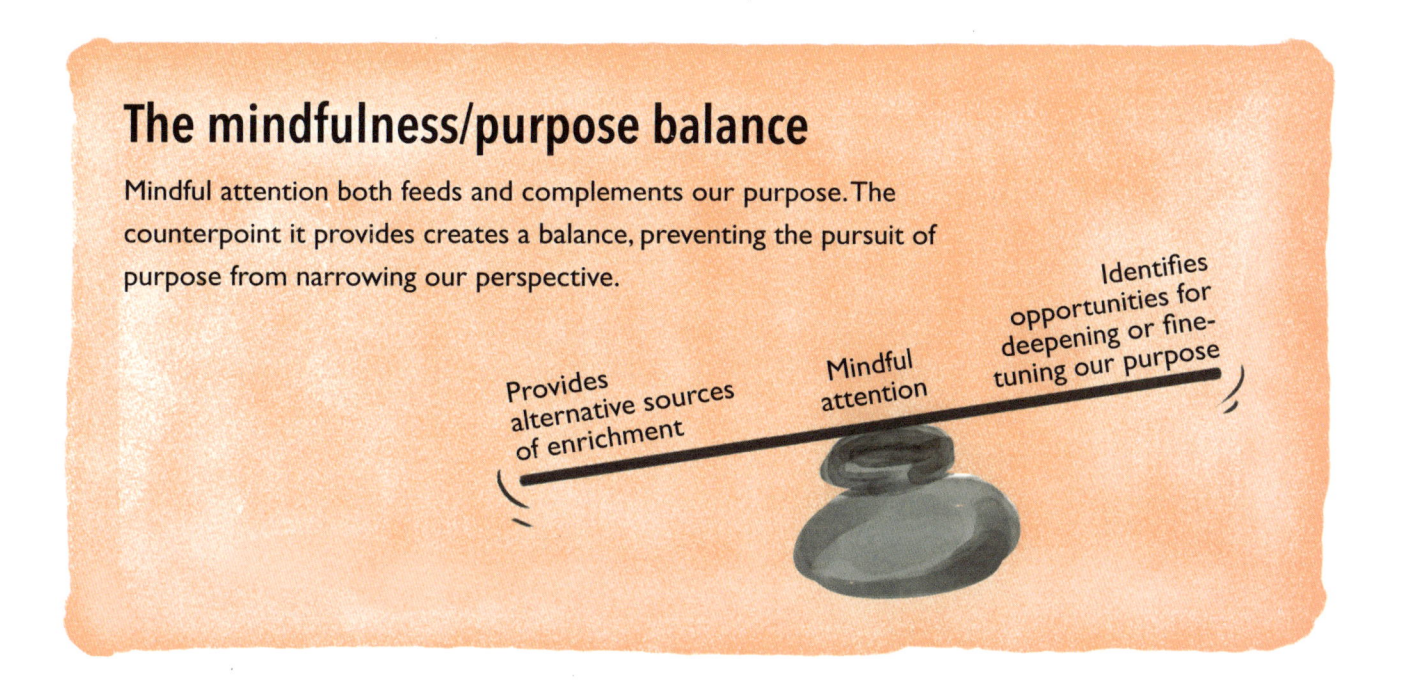

Mindful attention both feeds and complements our purpose. The counterpoint it provides creates a balance, preventing the pursuit of purpose from narrowing our perspective.

Provides alternative sources of enrichment

Mindful attention

Identifies opportunities for deepening or fine-tuning our purpose

LEARNING FROM HAIKU

Japan's most famous contribution to poetry is the haiku, the short verse (usually rendered in English as three lines) that aims to capture a moment of experience. Here is one from the poet Hekigodo Kawahigashi: 'From a bathtub/ I chuck water into the lake/ – a slight muddiness appears.' The everyday observation, sharp and meticulous, is presented without comment – just as a moment of mindfulness is experienced without judgment.

Being open to such phenomena, whether in nature, city streets or your own home, is undoubtedly fulfilling. Having a large-scale vision of the future brings a risk that you will miss what is happening now on a small scale. The haiku mentality provides an important corrective: stop and notice little everyday pleasures.

WORK AND FAMILY

FINDING YOUR OWN NORMS

There is absolutely no reason why anyone whose main purposes in life are work- and/or family-related should feel they are being timid or boring in following the mainstream – any more than a person who does *not* place the highest value on these matters should feel self-centred or freakish. To be happy need have nothing to do with being original.

When work is a motivating purpose, that usually comes from the sense of making a positive contribution and being part of a collective enterprise. Being valued by others and having sympathetic work colleagues help to make the experience positive. Working in a pleasant environment and doing something you believe is worthwhile also tend to boost satisfaction levels.

MAKING WORK WORK FOR YOU

However, there are many who find meaning in work even when they are frustrated in their jobs. Their purpose is then to remove the frustration – by persuading a boss to give them more or less responsibility, or a different role; by learning new skills to take them to the next level; or by finding a job elsewhere that suits them better.

Well-being is endangered when job frustration becomes woven into your experience and accepted as the norm. You complain profusely, and complaint becomes a leitmotif of your life, expected by friends and family. Mindfulness practice can help you see the harm this is causing and identify the appropriate steps to plan and commit to positive change.

If your career is going well, the principal risk is that it robs you of time you could otherwise spend on home life. Missing children growing up is a price often paid by the careerist – who ironically might be working hard for the family's prosperity. Such factors come into play as you rise in seniority, since bosses are often expected to work long hours. Remember: your boss is not alone in requiring your service. Your performance at home is not subject to formal review, and you may have the most sympathetic of partners. However, everyone should be aware of the personal cost of committing too much of your energy to your job. Take stock. Make any adjustments required.

To be happy yourself is an inestimable gift to your children.

FAMILY MATTERS

Many parents see self-sacrifice as essential to good parenting, and indeed it is: children must come first. However, it is important to offer to kids an example of a fully realized adult life. To be happy yourself is an inestimable gift to them. Within your overall purpose of serving your children, you can serve them well by sharing whatever gives you pleasure – or at least giving them plenty of opportunities to do so … and then not minding if they decline the invitation.

An often neglected aspect of parenting – and grandparenting – is noticing. To some extent children and parents lead parallel inner lives, even if their outer lives largely overlap. A parent needs to be alert to subtle indications that something might be amiss. Mental health issues are common among the young, and the sooner you become aware of any problem, the more likely it is to be resolved – perhaps without needing professional help.

THE ROLE OF CARER

Many of us become carers eventually – the less developed the social care system in your country, the more likely this is to happen. Your purpose then becomes clear, but clarity does not make the role of carer any easier. Empathy and patience will be required in abundance. You may feel your ikigai has morphed into bearing another person's life upon your shoulders. One important requirement is to fight against stereotyping: the helpless dependant and the all-capable carer. You need to recruit any available support and take respite on a regular basis. Keep your passions – your ikigai – alive, even if you have much less time for them now. Take pleasure in lovely moments of closeness, memory and whatever fun you can share – there will be good times if you remain open to the possibility.

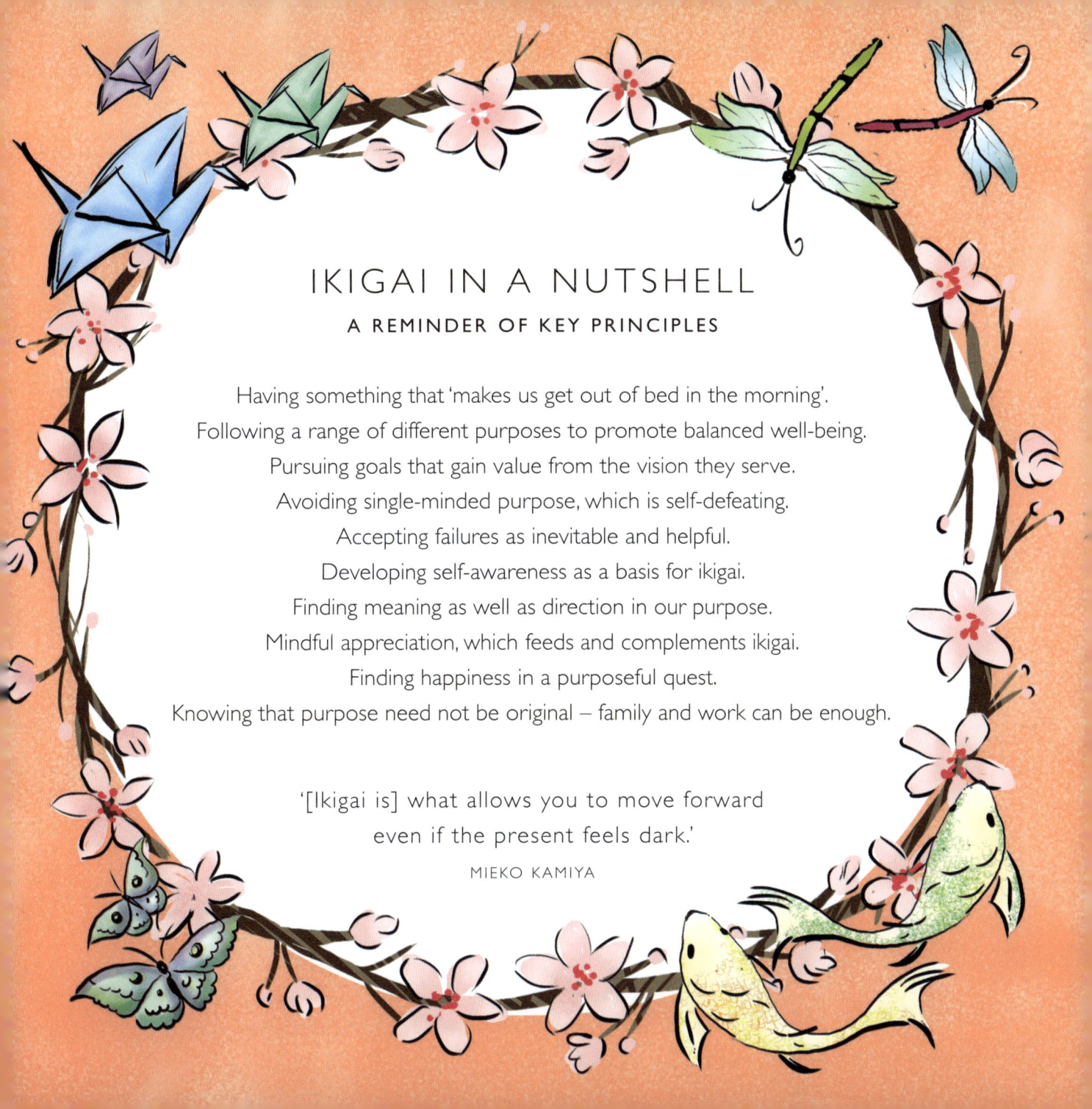

IKIGAI IN A NUTSHELL
A REMINDER OF KEY PRINCIPLES

Having something that 'makes us get out of bed in the morning'.
Following a range of different purposes to promote balanced well-being.
Pursuing goals that gain value from the vision they serve.
Avoiding single-minded purpose, which is self-defeating.
Accepting failures as inevitable and helpful.
Developing self-awareness as a basis for ikigai.
Finding meaning as well as direction in our purpose.
Mindful appreciation, which feeds and complements ikigai.
Finding happiness in a purposeful quest.
Knowing that purpose need not be original – family and work can be enough.

'[Ikigai is] what allows you to move forward
even if the present feels dark.'

MIEKO KAMIYA

CHAPTER SEVEN

LAGOM

How to find happiness by following the Swedish principle of lagom — a blend of balance, moderation, simplicity, fairness, good citizenship and being grateful for life's best gifts.

THE MIDDLE WAY

DOING THINGS IN MODERATION

Lagom (which rhymes with 'car-prom') came to prominence in 2017 as a traditional Swedish happiness concept to rival hygge, the Danish notion of mindful comfort and connection. The word means 'just the right amount', though its ramifications go further than that, since happiness is always multi-dimensional. Frugality, balance and fairness are all key ingredients.

Lagom is a mode of living – a philosophical framework that informs one's mindset. This encompasses, for example, the large question of life/work balance, for many a major preoccupation.

A Scandinavian overlap

Happiness concepts are not exclusive: one tradition often overlaps with another. Swedish lagom, in particular, shows some kinship with hygge, its Danish cousin, in the following shared values:

- Simplicity
- Nature
- Unpretentiousness

THE VALUE OF RESTRAINT

This is a value system that spurns extremity and excess, which puts it in tune with the modern emphasis on ecological sustainability. Not surprisingly, commercial interests have put their own profitable spin on this idea. For example, Ikea, the Swedish furniture company, created a 'Live Lagom' project to educate the public in greener living, with the help of gift vouchers handed out to customers, prompting them to buy Ikea products to help them save energy, reduce waste and live more healthily.

One proverbial phrase that to some extent captures lagom's ethos is: 'Less is more'. More important than frugality for its own sake, however, is appropriateness. The latter, of course, is subjective. Some would deem restraint to be appropriate in many circumstances – for example, when enjoying a snack, buying ornaments for a Christmas tree or renting a holiday cottage.

Lagom reflects to some extent an underlying tendency of the Swedish state: an emphasis on equality and consensus. Although the recession of the early 1990s prompted an increased tolerance of risk, the preference for modesty and moderation remained entrenched. This is a country where unions cooperate harmoniously with bosses, and where workers take their jobs seriously but go home on time to be with their families.

Since restraint is meaningful in design as well as lifestyle terms, it is not surprising that manufacturers have fashioned a set of aesthetics from lagom. Anything plain, unfussy or natural can be corralled under the lagom label, with a sprinkling of Scandinavian chic.

Frugality, balance and fairness are all key ingredients of lagom.

THE GOLDEN MEAN

In ancient Greek thought, especially the writings of Aristotle, the idea of the 'golden mean' between the two extremes of deficiency and excess was convincingly argued. Even virtues, according to this view, can be pushed beyond desirable limits. An example would be courage, which at the far end of the scale can turn to recklessness.

At various points in history, especially during the Romantic period, there were voices speaking out for the opposite opinion, even though today this seems self-indulgent. William Blake wrote that: 'The road of excess leads to the palace of wisdom.' The drug culture of 1960s hippiedom is a modern extension of this idea, which thrives today in many circles, and not only among the young. However, the dangers of such self-abuse are well known. The most obvious is addiction, with all its consequent damage to health and relationships. More subtle but equally negative is the harm delivered to the sense of the self as an active participant in society, contributing to (rather than undermining) the common good.

The simplest way of describing what intemperance threatens is in a single phrase: self-respect. In any society self-respect is dependent on self-control: a resistance to the siren lure of appetite and sensation.

> "It is best to rise from life as from a banquet – neither thirsty nor inebriated."
>
> *Aristotle*

BETWEEN ROCKS AND WHIRLPOOL

Swedes themselves are sometimes heard lamenting the importance attached to lagom in their culture. The problem with lagom, they say, with its emphasis on balance and harmony, is that these qualities can result in stasis and complacency. Lagom is not aspirational or progressive. Instead, it promotes the perpetual of established social norms.

There may be some truth in this view, but as with any belief system there is scope for a whole range of different interpretations. Anyone looking to Sweden for a possible roadmap towards happiness is entitled to take the best of lagom and leave aside any perceived shortcomings. Moderation may not sound like an inspiring watchword but steering a middle course is undoubtedly preferable to crashing on rocks in one direction or being sucked into a whirlpool in the other. What the rocks and whirlpool metaphorically represent is again a matter of interpretation. If the rocks are equivalent to taking extreme action and the whirlpool is doing nothing at all, then lagom will take you safely forward.

THE JOY OF SIMPLICITY

GOING BACK TO BASICS

To simplify is to strip things down to essentials, or at least discard some of the *in*essentials. As a lifestyle principle, this idea has much to recommend it. To venture the broadest possible generalization, there are two dimensions in which simplifying, or decluttering, can be beneficial: time and space.

FINE-TUNING TIME

Since time is finite we have to make countless decisions about how to handle it. Many of our everyday anxieties spring from having too much to do in too little time. Having an overlong to-do list is contrary to the spirit of lagom, since harmony and balance in our lives will escape us if we feel overstretched. Much of what we do is voluntary but we cannot necessarily rely on ourselves to act in our own best interests.

The most obvious demonstration of this is social media, which robs us of time we could otherwise be spending in real-life interactions. Even in the real world the question of how many friends it is feasible or rewarding to have is intriguing. Anyone who spends, say, three nights a week with different friends might protest a sense of entitlement: if this suits them, why should they worry? However, in matters of lifestyle we often drift into situations unconsciously, not questioning whether we would be happier if we made active choices to change them.

To free up valuable time you might also choose to eliminate any unnecessary commitments you have taken on. This, of course, will require you to re-evaluate your priorities – always a mentally healthy and refreshing exercise.

Mindfully rebalance your day

Effective time management is the subject of a well-established skill set, including such principles as prioritizing, delegating and setting boundaries. Below are some less obvious principles that will help you find space in your day for satisfying personal needs.

Early mornings

Do something creative early in the morning, perhaps over breakfast – anything from writing a journal to reading, or listening to an audio-book. It is worth getting up an hour early, at least once a week, to make this possible. Keep your early morning me-time a work- and anxiety-free zone. Try meditating as an alternative option.

Elevenses

Instead of grabbing a coffee on the go, visit a coffee shop. Use this time to read a newspaper or news feed, do a puzzle, or catch up on personal correspondence. If you freelance, the coffee shop makes a stimulating environment for working on your laptop for a couple of hours – mostly you will not be expected to have more than one coffee.

Lunch times

Make lunch a social occasion if you can. If you find social evenings are too long, too expensive or impossible owing to family ties, a good solution may be to see friends at lunchtimes, just for an hour, instead.

Afternoons

Mid-afternoon can be a flat and unproductive time. Save some of your most enjoyable chores for this period, by way of compensation. Also consider having a refreshing half-hour siesta.

Late evenings

Allow yourself a hour or so of me-time before you go to bed. Use this for cuddling your partner, watching TV, reading for pleasure or working on a personal project. Avoid tea, coffee or alcohol, and stay away from the kitchen store cupboard. An evening meditation can be a good preparation for sleep.

Mindful home decluttering

The little-by-little approach to decluttering seldom works, as you will probably become distracted from the project. Instead, set aside a whole day if you can and work hard at it. Take pride in your own efficiency. Reward yourself afterwards. If you have helpers, make a social occasion of the event, and treat everyone as a thank-you afterwards.

Relish relief
Decluttering is like filling in a tax form: it's a routine job you can put off for ages, and the longer you do, the more monstrous it becomes in your mind. Choose the right time, organize yourself with bin bags and so on, and tackle the job with relish.

Recycle
Find good homes if possible for anything you do not want. Otherwise, recycle responsibly, following the guidelines for your area. Minimize the amount of landfill you create.

Follow the three-year rule
If you have not used something for three years, you probably never will. Overcome your reservations and donate, recycle or throw out your 'just-in-case' items.

Make zones of emptiness
Organize your home so not every space is filled. Empty zones give you a sense of freedom. Avoid using liberated space as an overflow area for more stuff.

Decluttering removes the negative energies radiated by unwanted stuff.

SIMPLIFYING SPACE

The home is the other dimension where simplification is worthwhile. Clutter out of sight robs you of the opportunity to make more efficient use of storage because your cupboards are all full. Clutter on display – a profusion of object on surfaces – makes your routine cleaning a significantly bigger job. Decluttering removes the negative energies radiated by unwanted *stuff*. If this reference to 'energies' sounds questionable, bear in mind how uncomfortable you feel when you think about tidying left undone, and conversely how satisfying it is to complete a major clear-out.

INNER DETOX

PURIFYING YOUR LIFE

The deepest level of decluttering is purification, without any of the religious connotations associated with that word. We carry around with us an *inner* clutter, in our thoughts, habits and personalities: a tangle of emotions, anxieties and conditioned reflexes. The metaphor of 'baggage' is supremely apt. Much of our baggage seriously impedes us in our efforts to move through life. Purification helps to lighten it, allowing us to take wing.

A baggage audit

Our inner baggage is a jumble of negative or unhelpful thoughts and emotions beyond our control. Here is a list of the most common components, some overlapping. To purify yourself of all these tendencies is a major undertaking, possible through mindfulness meditation or some similar self-help discipline. For the moment, just spend quiet time mindfully thinking about which of these issues features in your psychological make-up and how and why they affect you. Once you have boosted your self-awareness, you can make positive choices to move forward instead of letting these tendencies hold you back.

Conditioned responses	**Regrets**	**Hurts caused by others**
Anxieties	**Low self-esteem**	**Disappointments**
Unwanted desires	**Low expectations**	

A five-step purification programme

These recommendations are a starting point for rebalancing. Focus on making progress in all five areas, then consider what further steps you can take to eliminate the negative from your life.

1. Look after your body
Make sure you get enough sleep and exercise. Eat and drink healthily – consider going vegetarian or vegan. Work to vanquish any addictions – to be successful in this, you will first need to understand *why* you have them.

2. Make space for love
Nourish your connections. If love is your priority, selfish urges will fall away, because love will always give you deeper and more lasting satisfactions.

3. Be true to yourself
Work to abolish any chasm between the private self and the public self. Stand up for what you believe in – but question it first, since automatic assumptions are often fallible.

4. Be thankful
Attend closely to the world's phenomena and be grateful for all creation. Show your thanks by deep engagement, especially with nature and other people. Savour the miracle of your existence – of being alive, here and now.

5. Meditate
A mindfulness meditation can help you to focus on principles 2, 3 and 4. Try meditation without worrying whether you are doing it right. Remember, your mind is bound to wander: if it does, just return your attention to the point of focus without being at all concerned.

HOW TO FIND BALANCE

LIVING HARMONIOUSLY

Variety in life provides us with a range of welcome stimuli. We often enjoy new experiences simply for their freshness – going to a new place or trying a new activity brings a *frisson* of joy, a pleasurable sense of a fresh experience. Much of what we do, however, is a matter of familiar actions in familiar places, often alternating between work and home, with excursions along well-trodden routes for shopping, errands and recreation.

Many people find sufficient variety – an amount that satisfies their particular personal needs – without consciously having to seek it. This will usually involve a range of interactions, environments and types of activity. Ideally, different rhythms will be experienced. There will be periods of intense activity (manual work, exercise and sports all spring to mind), followed by slower, quieter interludes (reading, writing, resting, walking, driving, watching TV). Another pattern, overlaid on fast and slow, will be indoors and outdoors, usually modified according to season. Moreover, there will be human configurations too – some things you do with selected others, some maybe in a team (at work or play), a few alone.

> "What is happiness except the simple harmony between a man and the life he leads?"
>
> *Albert Camus*

> **One of the symptoms of an approaching nervous breakdown is the belief that one's work is terribly important.**
>
> *Bertrand Russell*

MAKING CORRECTIONS

Within these different patterns it is easy for imbalances to set in, sometimes without your even being aware of it. One day a realization might dawn: you are not getting enough time with your family, or with friends, or it is weeks since you had any kind of encounter with nature. Some imbalances lend themselves to a quick fix – it is usually not too difficult to contrive a country walk, even if it means a drive or a train ride. Others are dangerously deep-rooted, particularly if they revolve around competing claims of home and work life, which many people juggle with difficulty, to the point of becoming stressed.

HOME AND WORK TENSIONS

Work usually takes us away from the home, and the longer the travelling time between the two, the less time we have for our loved ones. In extreme cases home might be seen as refuge, comfort, joy, meaning; work as tedium, subordination, frustration. If your situation comes anywhere close to this, your main priority will be to find ways to inject more satisfaction into what you do for a living. Exert as much influence as you can to ensure you are doing something fulfilling. Look for meaning in cooperation, in teamwork, and in working to the best of your ability. Equip yourself with new skills to enlarge your range of possibilities.

The other priority, for everyone who works, is to ensure you are not damaging your home life, your relationships and your health and well-being by workplace overload and stress. This is one of the most damaging forms of personal excess. You may believe that work pressures are beyond your control, that getting through a heavy load is what you are paid for. However, alongside your responsibility to your employer you have a responsibility to yourself and family. When work pressures narrow your life, causing you to sacrifice leisure pursuits or time spent with family or friends, stress and fatigue are reinforced – because the activities you have jettisoned are those that inject vitality. Mindfulness meditations can block this downward spiral by helping you to perceive where your best interests lie and make choices that are more consistent with them.

Avoid the trap of equating your job with your identity. Your job may be pressured, but that does not mean you need to take those pressures personally and be stressed by them. Stay detached, while giving your best efforts.

Mindfulness meditations can help you perceive where your best interests lie.

Warning signs at work – and how to address them

If you can tick any of the following experiences as applicable to your situation, you need to spend a mindful half-hour rethinking your priorities and coming up with a plan to create a more satisfactory home/work balance. This will be largely about adjusting attitudes, but in addition you will certainly need to make some concrete changes, especially in your time management.

- You often bring work home with you and do it in the evenings.
- You often think about work problems when you wake up in the night.
- You have missed significant family occasions on account of competing work responsibilities over the past year.
- You stay later at work than most of your colleagues.

Having analysed the problem, work on possible solutions. Here are some practical suggestions for breaking work's stranglehold:

- Aim to work more efficiently, to keep overload at bay.
- Draw more upon any resources available, including help from peers and juniors – or even bosses.
- Anticipate pressure points and lay down in advance effective ways of diffusing the stress.
- Scan your routines for time-wasting meetings or procedures and do your best to eliminate them.
- Work at home occasionally if it helps, to cut down on wasteful commuting time.

SELF AND OTHERS

SOCIAL LIVING

In Sweden the idea that every individual is integrated into civic society by mutual obligations is deep-rooted. Individualism has its place: without it there could be no creativity, no variation of personality. However, to push individualism too far is not the Swedish way. Instead there is a social fabric that depends on continual personal efforts for its upkeep. To break step would be wrong. Others would be disadvantaged, and that would be morally reprehensible. Moreover, a bad example would be set.

This translates into a strong sense of civic responsibility that discourages selfish or thoughtless action. Many laws against social disruption are easily and frequently broken. Take, for example, littering. Not to pick up your own litter is to stain the shared environment for the sake of avoiding a minor personal inconvenience. Being conscientious about litter is one of many requirements of the social contract that implicitly binds all citizens in a set of reciprocal responsibilities and benefits.

Preserving the common good

When everyone has equal and open access to a resource, it is easy for self-interested parties to find ways of exploiting the situation. For example, in a municipal garden, anyone can selfishly cut and collect flowers to display back home. Systems like this rely on conscience for their policing. In the spirit of lagom it would be unthinkable to pursue the path of personal advantage. When such a system is working smoothly, everyone's happiness is promoted.

Civic action mission statement

Here are some activities to consider as the basis for a personal programme of civic action that will strengthen your sense of being a contributing member of your society in the spirit of lagom. See if you can extend each list and perhaps think of further whole categories in which to exhibit social virtues.

The environment

- Controlling litter
- Closing gates
- Reporting damage
- Reducing carbon footprint
- Recycling

The neighbourhood

- Looking out for others
- Visiting elderly and sick neighbours
- Volunteering
- Mentoring
- Charitable giving

GOING FURTHER

However, anyone can go further in contributing to an unlittered environment. Occasionally, you might have seen someone combing a beach collecting other people's litter with a view to proper disposal. This is *lagom* taken to an admirable level of civic service. As with all selfless actions, knowing that you have exercised one of your cherished values and made a significant contribution is its own reward.

PRINCIPLES OF FAIRNESS

BEING EVEN-HANDED

Fairness covers such behaviour as playing by the rules, attending to other people's views and wishes, and patiently taking your turn. There is also the matter of justice. It would be unfair to judge someone without weighing the evidence and giving them an opportunity to defend themselves. It would also be unfair to exploit your connections for personal gain at another's expense.

Injustice all too often prevails at a personal, commercial or institutional level even in civilized societies. It can happen within a social group when someone is ostracized without knowing why; or in the professional realm when, say, an expert overcharges someone who desperately needs their services and cannot walk away. If you witness such behaviour there is a moral imperative to speak out against the unfairness and maybe lend your support to its victims. This can be taken as far your conscience dictates and your energy and time allow. Social activism – even if it amounts to no more than signing petitions – is an ennobling gift from the heart, offering a fine example to others.

THE PERSONAL LEVEL

Whenever you give someone the benefit of the doubt, you are invoking the judicial principle of 'innocent until proven guilty'. In the everyday world this includes declining to participate in gossip – a mode of communication intrinsically unfair. Thinking the best of people may lead at times to disappointment – that is a better outcome that knowing you have done someone a disservice. The regret attached to over-harsh judgments is not easily expunged.

EQUAL TREATMENT

Another aspect of fairness is not showing bias or favouritism in situations where even-handedness is more appropriate. Obviously a teacher or employer should follow this principle, and a parent who favours one child rather than another is potentially doing psychological harm. In other kinds of relationship the ethics might not be so clear-cut, but a useful guide is intuition. Another lodestone is the idea of extending to others the allowance you would regard yourself as warranting if you were in the same position.

Dimensions of fairness

In deciding whether you are being fair, or someone is treating you fairly, consider these different nuances of fairness. In the public realm, differences of opinion about which of these aspects is most important lead to policy differences between states and political parties.

Equality
Even-handed treatment regardless of need or deservedness.

Deservedness
Rewarding positive qualities, such as ability, effort or virtue.

Need
Giving benefits to those most in need of them – for example, the haves giving to the have-nots.

THE ART OF APPRECIATION

BEING GRATEFUL FOR LIFE'S BEST GIFTS

Our lives tend to be full of clutter and distraction. Clutter *is* distracting, because it provides an unwanted focus to which our thoughts will often steer themselves on auto pilot. Clearing out our *external* clutter, the stuff that fills our home, as well as starting to face and resolve our *internal* confusions (anxieties, self-doubts, habitual emotional responses), can bring relief and refreshment. Reorganizing our time to focus on our true priorities is also deeply healing. Once you have been through these cleansing processes you are better placed than ever to truly appreciate life's finest pleasures.

TEMPERATE ENJOYMENT

The 17th-century Dutch philosopher Baruch Spinoza argued that a temperate life need not be so fiercely ascetic as to banish pleasure. 'Nothing forbids our pleasure,' he wrote, 'but a savage and sad superstition. For why should it be more proper to relieve our hunger and thirst than to rid ourselves of melancholy?' To be temperate is to enjoy better – not less. Whereas the intemperate person is a slave to their appetites, the temperate individual exercises choice wisely to savour the best experiences available.

To have insatiable desires is a kind of malady of the imagination. If acted upon, such desires leading to pointless self-indulgence – 'pointless' because attempting to increase our pleasure incrementally, each time taking a bigger bite, never raises our level of satisfaction. Instead, we just become jaded. The connoisseur, by contrast, favours quality over quantity, the object itself not the sensation of consuming it.

DIMENSIONS OF PLEASURE

These thoughts about temperance apply particularly to the pleasures of the body – eating, drinking, making love. In the same category is the quest for an adrenaline high – derived, for example, from speed or danger. However, extremes can be found in every realm of life, including art and nature.

The nature lover might dream of a visit to the Grand Canyon as the ultimate experience of landscape. There is, of course, nothing wrong with liking or visiting dramatic places. However, everyday contentment could be said to involve appreciating what is near at hand rather than constantly aspiring to an elsewhere. There will be always something wonderful to enjoy within your own orbit, although the pleasures on offer may be subtle or low-key.

To be grateful for life's local pleasures is a more enriching approach than thinking they are inadequate to your needs or tarnished by over-familiarity.

THE PATH OF GRACE

BEING YOUR BEST SELF

Of all human characteristics, grace is one of the most difficult to define. People who show grace seem to be blessed, as if divinely. They somehow attain excellence without any striving. However, this impression does not take us any closer to what 'grace' actually means.

Graceful people have a quiet charisma, with depths of compassion, love, humour and courage continually in reserve. They exude moral authority, without being solemn or judgemental. They always seem to do and say the right thing, and would never commit a careless *faux pas*. This does not mean they are immune to mistakes, only that any mistakes they do make are understandable and that they accept responsibility for them and learn from them.

There is no set of clear prescriptions for being graceful, since the quality is based on the whole self, reasonably well adjusted to its circumstances – any issues are mindfully understood, with choices in place for tackling them. However, it is plausible to identify three foundation stones for grace:

Self-care: Being good to yourself, and taking a serious approach to your health and well-being (including your moral and spiritual well-being), is essential.

Patience: Slowing down, and taking any challenge step by step, without being overwhelmed by its dimensions, is part of grace too.

Kindliness: This is more than kindness: it involves being perpetually well-disposed towards people in general, as well as open-hearted and giving.

Some further qualities of grace are suggested in the box opposite.

EVERYDAY BEAUTY

Despite fashion journalism's fondness for the word, serious-minded people would claim that grace is nothing to do with beauty. In truth, however, grace gives beauty to anyone who possesses it, even if they do not conform to conventional norms of body shape or facial appearance. To live gracefully is to create your own beauty through the way you live. We can all do this if we can rid ourselves of our insecurities and attachments, and in the process we are likely to find happiness, and even spread it into the lives of others.

Elements of grace

Anyone who has all the characteristics listed below is blessed indeed. Think of someone you know who has all or most of these characteristics and take inspiration from the way they carry themselves and relate to others.

Courtesy	Prudence	Temperance	Courage	Humility
Fairness	Compassion	Generosity	Gratefulness	Simplicity
Open-mindedness	Gentleness	Humour	Love	

> *Remember the golden eternity is yourself.*
>
> — Jack Kerouac

CONFIDENT HUMILITY

BEING QUIETLY STRONG

Boasting, arrogance, self-important swagger and all other forms of egotism disrupt social harmony and distort relationships. An egotist may even believe that the world revolves around himself or herself. This can be accurate in some cases, since the me-centred view is self-determining, but it is always a damaging syndrome. In truth, everyone's life is a side-show, however urgent or compelling the dramas played out on our particular stage.

The opposite of boastfulness is shrinking humility: the belief that nothing you can do makes a difference. This mindset is equally misguided. A healthy society is one in which all know they can make a difference, either by individual action or, more usually, by working cooperatively with others.

The most admirable form of humility has nothing to do with undervaluing the self. It is based instead on understanding your powers and limits in any situation. This makes it a kind of wisdom, from which positive, quietly confident actions – and a happy life – are more likely to spring.

Quiet confidence starts with identifying a realistically achievable purpose and moving forward to attain it despite any setbacks along the way. Self-knowledge is an essential starting point – understanding how to exploit your strengths and minimize or work around your weaknesses. It is acceptable to take pride in your successes but you must avoid the pitfall of thinking you can always do everything alone. Asking for help when you need it – including emotional support – is not a reflection of inadequacy.

A mindful plan for confidence

Most people feel perfectly relaxed among family and friends. However, it is common to lose confidence in situations where you are feel you are being judged – even if you are not – or where the possibility of failure is so scary it undermines your efforts. Mindfulness (see pages 28–31 and 178–181) offers us a way to deal with confidence lapses. It helps us see our unjustified reasons for self-doubt, minimize negative self-talk and shift the focus to the positive. It makes it less likely that we will shy away from challenge. Here are some key principles:

Accept mistakes
Do not waste energy in regret. Treat each mistake as an opportunity to learn and grow.

Inhabit your intention
Focus on your goal for its own sake rather than as a way to compensate for past errors.

Be true to yourself
Self-awareness and commitment to your values make it easier to find and exploit your potential.

Exercise your talents
If you have gifts, it would be wasteful not to use them – even if others do not appreciate your skills.

Make a contribution
Knowing you have made a difference will enhance your self-esteem.

NO ASSUMPTIONS

Being unassuming is a quality worth taking literally, by shedding unhelpful assumptions. Arrogance is often built on shaky premises – for example, the idea that you can win people over by charm or intelligence alone, or by emphatically stating your wishes. The mindful person tests all assumptions before acting on them. That is one way to minimize the unhappiness that springs from failed expectations.

The Ashanti people of West Africa have a proverb: 'No one tests the depth of a river with both feet.' Prudence also has a place in quiet confidence. Its various connotations include being careful what you say, protecting your resources, assessing levels of risk and making necessary preparations. None of this needs to imply timidity. You can be an adventurer, and that for you is where happiness might lie, but taking along maps and mosquito repellant is a precaution that makes it likelier you will live to tale your tales.

> "We come nearest to the great when we are great in humility."
>
> *Rabindranath Tagore*

LAGOM IN A NUTSHELL
A REMINDER OF KEY PRINCIPLES

'Just the right amount' – neither too much nor too little.
Avoiding waste – and helping to preserve the planet.
Following a healthy life/work balance.
Avoiding ostentation or attention-seeking.
Valuing the near-at-hand rather than looking only elsewhere for fulfilment.
Enjoying pleasures for their quality, not their quantity.
Prioritizing accurately, to deal with overload or conflicting responsibilities.
Finding harmony in life, and simplifying when that helps.
Being fair to others – resisting bias or prejudice.
Acting conscientiously for the common good.
Being modestly confident, avoiding arrogant assumptions.

'To go beyond is as wrong as to fall short.'
CONFUCIUS

CHAPTER EIGHT
TIBETAN BUDDHISM

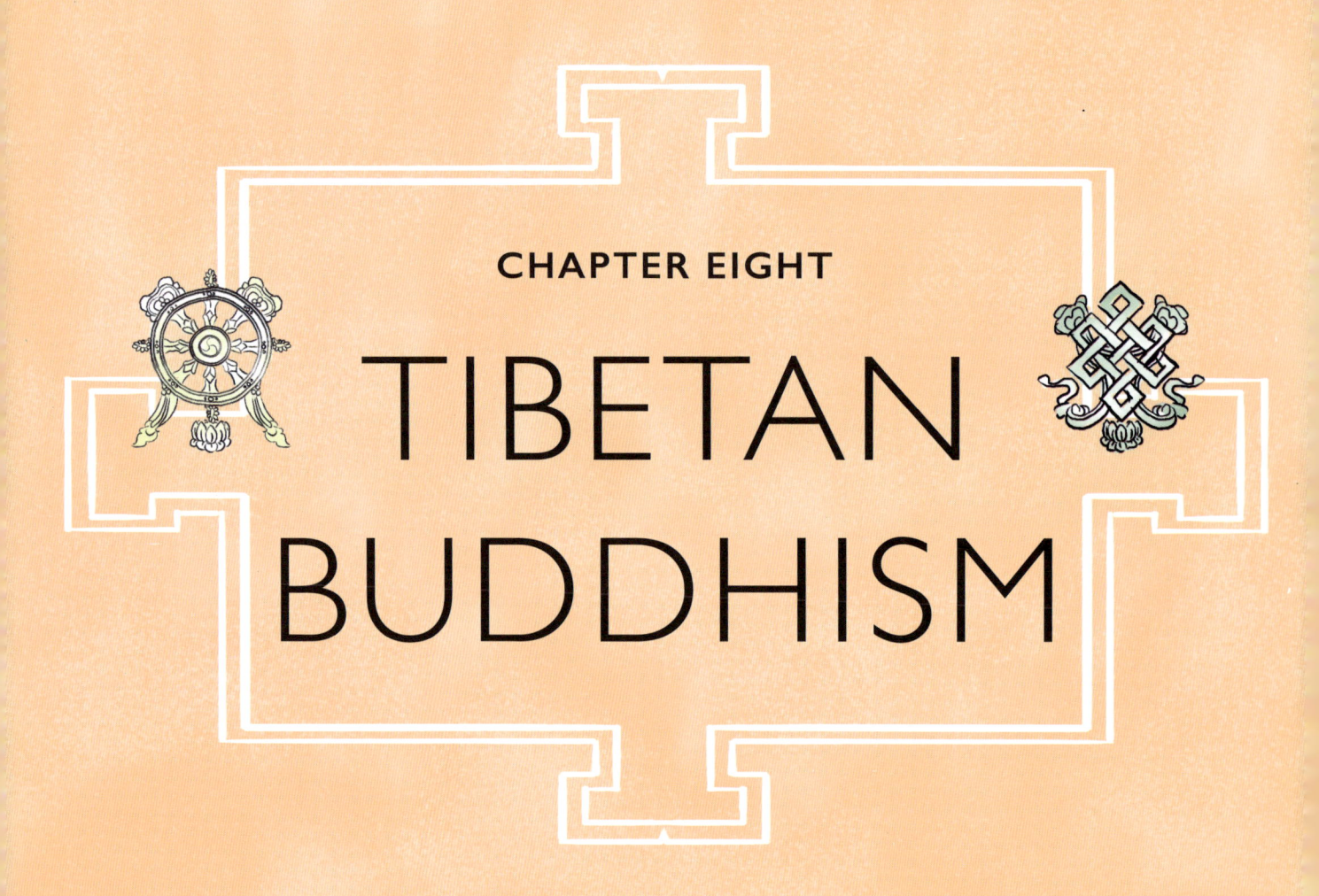

How to find happiness by learning the wisdom of the Buddha, mindfully following the way of compassion, letting go of our cravings and committing to regular meditation.

THE BUDDHA'S TEACHINGS

LIVING WITHOUT ILLUSION

His Holiness the Fourteenth Dalai Lama is one of the most recognizable people on the planet, and the most celebrated Buddhist. His radiant smile and sense of fun are infectious, but at the same time he has an air of profound wisdom and compassion. These are quintessentially Buddhist qualities. Many in the West have been inspired in recent decades by His Holiness and by other charismatic spiritual teachers to take aspects of Buddhism into their own hearts and lives.

The Four Noble Truths

The core of the Buddha's teachings is the Four Noble Truths:

- All existence is suffering (dukkha).
- The cause of suffering is desire, or craving.
- Suffering will cease when craving ceases.
- The way to end suffering is to follow the Noble Eightfold Path.

The Noble Eightfold Path is often represented as the eight spokes of the wheel of Dharma (teachings):

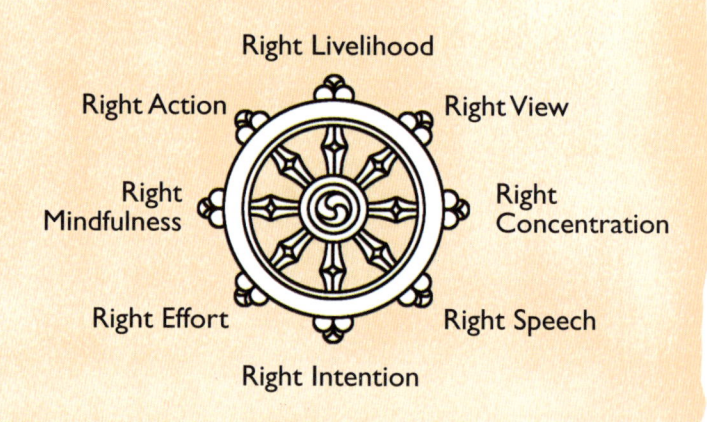

- Right Livelihood
- Right Action
- Right View
- Right Mindfulness
- Right Concentration
- Right Effort
- Right Speech
- Right Intention

ANCIENT WISDOM

Buddhism is a belief system dating back 2,500 years. Siddhartha Gautama Buddha, now usually known as the Buddha, was a Hindu prince who turned his back on luxury in a quest for truth. Then he spent much of his life (c.563–c.483 BCE) teaching in northern India. He never claimed to be a god or a prophet: he was simply an immensely wise mortal who gained insights into the meaning of life and the causes of human distress. The name 'Buddha' means the 'awakened one' – reflecting the fact that, through meditation, he attained enlightenment, or nirvana. This brings escape from the endless cycle of reincarnation. It is also unconditional happiness, in which the mind is liberated from disturbing emotions and expresses itself in peace, joy and compassion.

Inspired to deep thought by encountering, on a series of chariot rides, a sick man, an old man, a dead man and a monk, the Buddha renounced his worldly life as prince, husband and father and committed himself to the path of holiness. From the age of 29, he spent six years in ascetic practices to subdue body and mind, but meditation proved more fruitful than self-harm. His deepest insights came to him while meditating under the renowned Bodhi (pipal) tree. Later he acquired a handful of disciples and preached the famous sermon in the deer park near Sarnath – later known as the 'first turning of the wheel of the Dharma' (teachings). This was the beginning of his 45-year career as a teacher. He never wrote anything, but his teachings, committed to memory by various monks, were collected in due course as the sutras – the Buddhist scriptures.

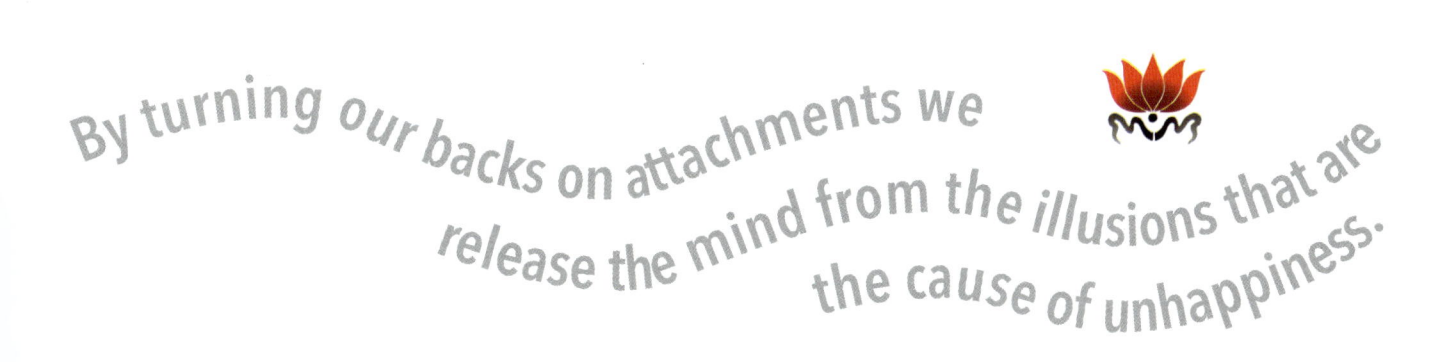

By turning our backs on attachments we release the mind from the illusions that are the cause of unhappiness.

TOWARDS THE TRUTH

The Buddha had no truck with doctrine. Instead, he sought to teach humankind a practical way to deal with the burden of suffering. Key to this was letting go of the 'attachments' we tend to cling to in our weakness – for example, pleasure, comfort and longing. All attachments are illusory because in time they fail to deliver, their satisfactions fading into oblivion. By turning our backs on them we release the mind from the illusions that are the cause of unhappiness. As we become more aware and more realistic about life, we attain peace of mind.

"In the end these things matter most: How well did you love? How deeply did you learn to let go?"

The Buddha

Traditions of Buddhism

Those who heeded the Buddha's teachings and took them into their hearts fall into distinct traditions, corresponding with different varieties of Buddhism still practised in the world today:

Theravada (Teaching of the Elders)
Theravada teachings focus on cause and effect (karma), as well as encouraging meditation as a way to distance yourself from troublesome thoughts and emotions.

By developing self-awareness and inner peace you are free to lead a good life and accumulate positive karma. These teachings spread through south-east Asia (especially Sri Lanka, Thailand, Cambodia and Burma).

Mahayana (Great Way)
Mahayana teachings, in the Northern Buddhist tradition, emphasize compassionate service to others and the attainment of wisdom. This is the dominant form of Buddhism in China, Japan and Tibet. The different schools include the Japanese Tendai and Pure Land, as well as Zen.

Also within the Mahayana tradition is Tibetan Buddhism, which embraces many different sets of practice. This strand of belief is commonly called Vajrayana, or the Diamond Way. It has a strong element of ritual, derived from Indian Tantra, a form of mystical Buddhism. A key element is the view that the mind has innate potential perfection.

RIPPLES OF CONSEQUENCE

CULTIVATING KARMA

Karma is one of Buddhism's best-known concepts. It reflects the popular wisdom: 'What we reap, we sow.' By positive action we usually generate a measure of well-being – for ourselves as well as the obvious beneficiaries. Our behaviour creates outcomes consistent with its underlying intention. If you harm somebody you bring suffering upon them but also, at some deeper level, upon yourself.

In traditional Buddhism karma is tied up with a belief in reincarnation. What we think, say and do plants karmic 'seeds', or energy traces, and the unfolding of these may appear at once or later – even in a future lifetime. According to Eastern thought we are born with – indeed because of – karma generated in past lives.

A belief in reincarnation is not a necessary precondition of benefiting from the law of karma. We know from experience how some small misdemeanour – a lie, a snippet of information unfairly given or withheld – can have consequences that compromise not just one relationship but several. Karma encourages us to take greater responsibility for our actions if they are deliberately or unwittingly negative. If, on the other hand, we do something rooted in virtuous intentions – generosity, compassion, forgiveness – the result is *positive* karma: a rainbow ripple that spreads benefits in all directions, including back towards ourselves.

Karma encourages us to take greater responsibility for our actions if they are deliberately or unwittingly negative.

MICRO EFFECTS

To think in tune with karma is to be aware of nuances. If you say something that is not quite what you mean, being misunderstood can put you in karmic deficit if your listener responds by being hurt or acting against their own interests. Your *faux pas*, of course, was not malicious, but this does not entirely excuse you in karmic terms. The lesson is: be alert to your karmic footprints. They may seem shallow, but their impact can be greater than at first you might imagine.

How to be a karmic hero

The karmic hero's skill is to achieve great things with no great effort – just an intention to add to happiness in countless small ways. The benefit achieved will outweigh the sacrifice made.

Spread your smile Smiling illustrates the basic karmic idea that small things can make a big difference. Distribute your smile widely – at home, in the workplace, wherever you travel.

Perform acts of kindness Small sacrifices, such as helping people with heavy shopping or giving up your seat on a train, are karmically beneficial.

Be secretly virtuous Good deeds do not require an audience. Generate good karma unseen.

Say nice things A complimentary remark can make people feel better about themselves, and can even make a person's day.

HOW TO CONQUER UNHAPPINESS

USING MIND POWER

Tibetan Buddhism places great importance on mind power. Our bodies deteriorate and we accommodate ourselves as best we can to physical decline. The mind too can deteriorate, disabling our capacity for making informed choices. However, for as long as our thinking remains lucid, we have a tremendous tool at our disposal – one we can use to rise above suffering and enter inner peace.

Actually, we may not be fully aware of our pain. It is there in our disappointments, our unsatisfied desires, our griefs, our fears about ageing. True, there is more to life than pain, but pleasure has its downside too, for it fades quite quickly to nothing. That is because, as well as suffering, life is characterized by impermanence. When we lose something or someone, we tend to cling even harder to what we have, but that only exacerbates our problem: our perpetual striving based on the illusion that happiness is the satisfaction of our desires.

THE PATH OF PEACE AND LOVE

Despite his dark-tinted view of life, the essential message of the Buddha is optimistic. Although life is suffering, there is a path of release we can follow while still alive. The lesson is to take a realistic view of life's pain and impermanence, release ourselves from illusion and desire, purify mind and heart, and focus on leading a life of peace, altruism and love. In the West, the Dalai Lama's teachings, as well as those of other spiritual leaders including Thich Nhat Hanh, have brought these precepts into the mainstream of mind-body-spirit thinking.

The Dalai Lama has said he believes the whole purpose of life is to seek happiness through training the 'mind' – he means not merely the intellect, but also intuition (heart) and the psyche (spirit). Accepting that life is fleeting allows us to relax our grip on it. When we avoid desperately clinging to transitory experiences, we free ourselves to care for what matters to us in a relaxed and compassionate way, with love.

LESSONS OF IMPERMANENCE

Understanding with all our mental capacities how fleeting life is encourages us to give due weight to some other basic truths about life. These are:

- It is precious to live in the moment – the insight of mindfulness.
- Change makes possible learning and spiritual growth.
- Love and compassion are infinitely more worthwhile than pleasure.
- Peace comes from acceptance of deep truths.

Despite his dark-tinted view of life, the essential message of the Buddha is optimistic.

THE PATH OF MINDFULNESS

BANISHING DISTRACTIONS

Mindfulness as a modern practice is well established in the West, but its roots lie in Buddhism. The Buddha regarded mindfulness as the path to enlightenment. As the Vietnamese monk Thich Nhat Hanh has written, 'Living mindfully and with concentration, we see a deeper reality and are able to witness impermanence without fear, anger or despair.'

No such thing as self

The Buddha developed a mental practice we now call 'insight meditation', or *vipassana*. It is based on the idea that unhappiness can be eliminated when we understand our true nature. Its purpose is to train the mind, by meditating on your body or its sensations, specifically your breathing, to be clear about the nature of reality, and in particular suffering, impermanence and 'non-self'. This latter term refers to the idea that there is no such thing as a permanent self: instead we have changing qualities. Believing in the self, or ego, makes us fall into cravings, which cause unhappiness. Understanding 'non-self', through meditation, enables us to still our desires and attain wisdom and peace.

STILLING THE MIND

Everyone's waking mind is continually abuzz with thoughts, flowing into and across each other in kaleidoscopic patterns which are largely random, even when we try to concentrate. This is what Buddhists call the 'monkey mind'. It is also the 'ego mind', since anxiety and unhappiness spring from our egotistic weaknesses – in particular, our craving for outcomes that do nothing to foster our well-being.

Mindfulness meditation is a channelling of the mind towards a specific focus – even our thoughts themselves, or our own breathing, or something external such as a mandala (spiritual pattern). The aim of mindfulness meditation is to make the mind stable and peaceful. Deepening our practice, we start to see that tranquillity, not confusion, is the mind's natural state. Through mindfulness we are bringing to light a quality always intrinsically present. We discover our birthright of peace and contentment.

The following two options are equally valid. You could find a school of Buddhism that appeals to you, and join a meditation class with an appropriate teacher. Or without preparation you could try a simple meditation practice as described on pages 30 and 181. Bear in mind you can benefit from mindfulness without having to subscribe to any nuances of Buddhist belief.

> "All that we are is a result of what we have thought."
>
> *The Buddha*

FIRST STEPS IN MEDITATION

CALMING THE MIND

The practice of calming the mind, common to many different traditions of Buddhism, is called *samatha*, which literally means 'calm'. Below is a simple step-by-step meditation that focuses on the sensations of your breathing. If you have never meditated before, you may feel somewhat daunted by the prospect. However, such feelings are unnecessary, for there is nothing difficult or esoteric about meditation. Many people worry they are not doing it right, but any such self-judgment is inappropriate to mindfulness. Just make a start, and keep doing it: the many benefits – heightened awareness, better concentration, less stress – will come unnoticeably over time.

Meditation misconceptions

Many people are reluctant to try meditation because they misunderstand its true nature. The following myths are particularly common:

- ♦ Meditation is a relaxation technique, akin to self-hypnosis.
- ♦ You need to have a spiritual mindset or be capable of deep philosophical thinking.
- ♦ Meditators exert firm control over their thoughts.
- ♦ You need to be able to sit cross-legged on the floor.
- ♦ You must acquire the skill of emptying your mind.

MEDITATE ON YOUR BREATHING

This simple practice, one of the cornerstones of mindfulness, aims to make you aware, in the moment, of an everyday natural process you normally take for granted.

1. In a quiet room, sit on a comfortable straight-backed chair with your feet flat on the floor, legs uncrossed. The base of your spine should be gently touching the chair back.
2. Lower your gaze so it falls unfocused a metre or so in front of you; or close your eyes if you prefer. Rest your hands palms down on your thighs.
3. Relax your body and your mind as much as possible, while staying alert. If you have trouble relaxing, just move to the next step without worrying about it.
4. Focus your attention on your breath – the sensations of each in-breath and out-breath wherever they are most apparent. For example, you could focus on the rise and fall of your belly, or the sensation of air entering and leaving your nose. Breathe normally, not unusually deeply.
5. If you mind wanders, return your focus gently to your breathing, without judging yourself for inattention.
6. Conclude your meditation after around five minutes. Open your eyes if you have closed them, and take in the features of the room. If you wish, you can use a timer, although some people find this spoils the mood.

The many benefits of meditation – heightened awareness, better concentration, less stress – will come unnoticeably over time.

THE COMPASSIONATE HEART

NOURISHING KINDNESS

In Mahayana Buddhism, which includes the Tibetan school, emphasis is placed on selfless sacrifice for the sake of others. The ultimate incarnation of this is the *bodhisattva*: the Buddhist who delays their own enlightenment (escape from the endless cycle of rebirth) to help others attain the same goal.

In the West we think of wisdom as intellectual and compassion as emotional, and the two as distinct from each other, but Buddhism sees things otherwise. For the Buddha, compassion stemmed from insight, and vice versa. Wisdom (*prajna*) and compassion (*karuna*) are like the two wings of a bird: without both there is no flight.

The perfection of giving

So natural and necessary is giving that Buddhists perceive it as non-hierarchical: 'no giver, no receiver'. This is why begging monks receive alms silently and give no thanks. We would do well to think of giving as a passage of spirit from each to the other. Givers and receivers create each other, and neither is superior to the other. On the other hand, gratitude is an important courtesy, and most receivers will want to express their thanks, sincerely and without ostentation.

INNER LIGHTNESS

If we accept there is no such thing as the self, the boundaries between one person and another dissolve into universal kinship. Selflessness becomes utterly logical. This is not merely philosophizing: when you behave selflessly you feel an inner lightness. If you are mindful of your experience, you will feel an inner liberation, a glow of contentment.

Compassion in Buddhism is not an emotion, more an aspiration – to relieve others of unhappiness. Wisdom enables us to understand suffering; empathy tells us how it feels. Cultivated as an instinct of the heart, compassion extended to those who need it is woven into our personality, even our identity. We should not expect thanks: all we are doing is acting in harmony with our own selves.

The loving kindness meditation

This practice begins with *self*-compassion – accepting yourself with all your oddities and flaws – and continues in growing circles to encompass others in love. Thus we add to the sum-total of happiness, including our own.

Sit in your usual meditation position and relax your mind and body.

Send kind, loving thoughts inwards to yourself. Imagine your whole self being suffused in self-generated compassion.

Visualize half a dozen people in turn and send them kind, loving energy, as rays from your heart. Start with those dear to you and progress by diminishing stages of closeness, concluding with someone who dislikes you.

SOUND POWER

WORKING WITH MANTRAS
The Buddha taught the dangers of becoming attached to rites, and many in the West will sympathize. However, ritual has a place in modern life, even among those who have no great religious conviction – just think of funerals, birth ceremonies, even blowing out candles on someone's birthday. All schools of Buddhism subscribe to the recitation of liturgical texts, or chanting. Moreover, continuously repeating a mantra – a sacred syllable or series of syllables – is a well-known meditation technique.

THE SINGING LOTUS
Perhaps the most famous mantra is *Om mani padme hum*, associated with Tibetan Buddhism. *Om* is a sacred Sanskrit syllable and *hum* expresses the spirit of enlightenment. *Mani padme* approximately means the 'Jewel of the Lotus'. Taken together, the mantra encapsulates, symbolically, a profound Buddhist truth: that by our actions and our insights we can transform our impure body, speech and mind into the Buddha's pure body, speech and mind – reflected in the three separate syllables of *om*: A-U-M.

Chanting the mantra *om* on its own is often practised as way of expressing what a Buddhist might call the 'eternal song of the Divine'. It is believed to bring peace, protection and abundance into your life. Moreover, it generates an aura of spiritual light around you, elevating you to a higher state of consciousness.

"Truly to sing, that is a different breath."

Rainer Maria Rilke

Join the chant

The mantra syllable *om* can be uttered silently, but if you are sitting still and at peace with others it is effective to create an audible vibration that is generated and experienced by all. Many would see this as a collective healing energy. Even if you have not yet accepted any version of Buddhist belief, it is worth experimenting with this mantra as a technique for inducing calm togetherness. Mantra meditation has been shown to lower blood pressure and heart rate, lower anxiety and stress, and heighten well-being.

- **Sit in a circle**, facing inwards. Choose one of the group as the conductor who sets the pace initially, prompting the others to join in.
- **Chant A-U-M.** You should feel the mantra's vibrations in your lower belly – if you cannot, try sitting up straighter.
- **Continue repetitively**, attending to the sounds in their slow, insistent rhythm to the exclusion of everything else. Think of the pattern of sound as a great protective canopy and each of yourselves as tent poles, keeping it in place.

Om mani padme hum

ༀ་མ་ཎི་པ་དྨེ་ཧཱུྂ།

PICTURE POWER

WORKING WITH MANDALAS
Another characteristic strand of Tibetan Buddhism is the practice of creating and meditating on a mandala. This is an artwork or graphic image that is rich in symbolic meaning. Often it takes the form of a painting, although the image can also be produced ephemerally in coloured grains of sand. Tibetans find deep spiritual value in creating a sand mandala, then brushing the sand away after use in a symbolic acceptance of impermanence and the importance of non-attachment.

A SACRED MAP
Mandalas were originally devised as a kind of sacred map of the cosmos. Tibetan examples portray a panoply of deities, while the Hindu tradition features a geometrical pattern of interlocking triangles, known as the Sri Yantra. The psychologist Carl Jung saw such designs as a potential tool for self-development, and this is perhaps why mandalas nowadays form such a popular genre of mind-body-spirit publishing, of which the latest manifestation is the mandala colouring book.

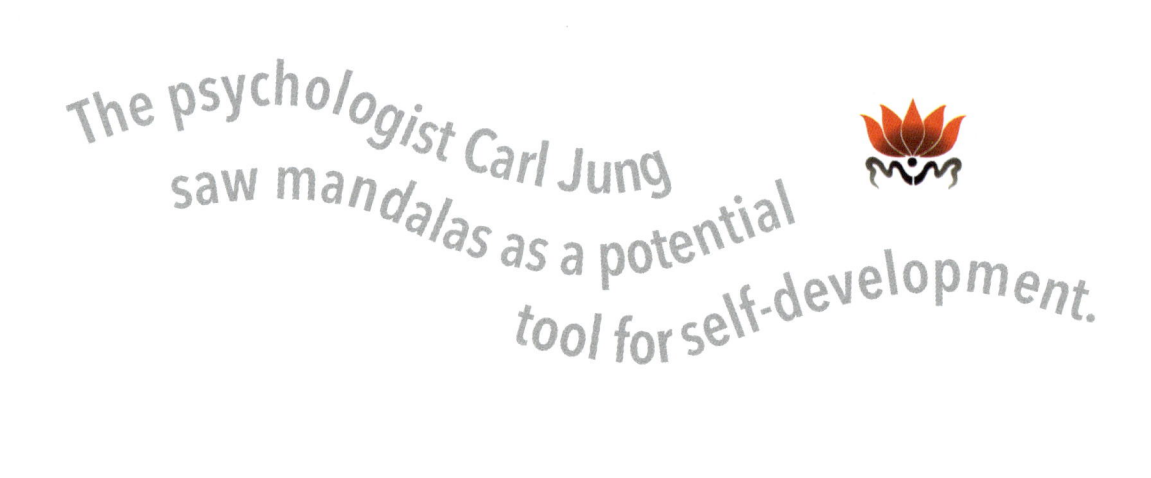

The psychologist Carl Jung saw mandalas as a potential tool for self-development.

Voyage to the centre

Serious mandala meditation can deepen your awareness of the true nature of reality. The ideal is to experience pure being, with no thoughts of past or future, no emotion and no exertion of the rationalizing brain. Undertaken regularly, such meditation can boost your confidence and resilience, hone your concentration and make you more accepting of chance's ups and downs. It can also reduce your stress level. Try the following improvised version of mandala meditation and see if it suits you better than meditating on your breath.

Use different circular lids and the like as stencils (or a set of compasses if you have one) for drawing a pattern of four concentric rings on a sheet of paper. Between these lines, draw simple outlines of people, flowers and stars – one in each of the three layers.

Draw a small circle at the centre of your image and fill it in.

Meditate on the layers of existence you have drawn, progressing inwards: humanity, nature, the cosmos.

Meditate on the image as sheer pattern, without any representational meaning. Attend mindfully to the lines on the paper, and nothing else.

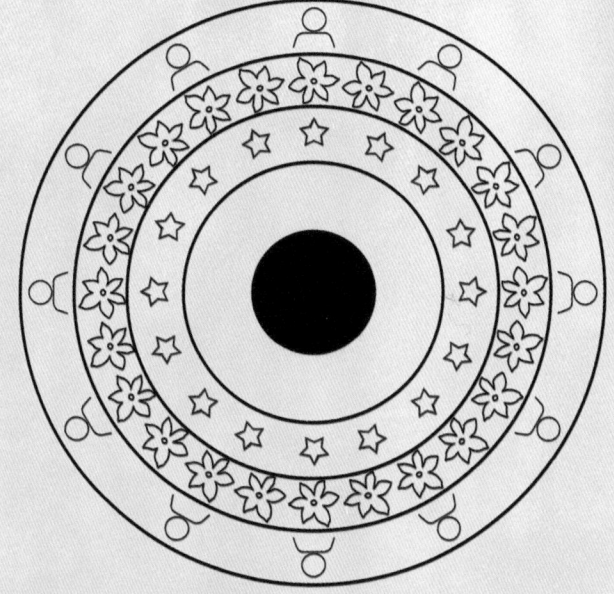

Turn your attention to the central 'hole'. Visualize yourself passing into this mystery to enter pure being. Just 'be here now', as the spiritual guru Ram Dass has put it.

THE INTEGRATED LIFE

GOING FURTHER

Buddhism's appeal in the West reflects its emphasis on peace, mindfulness and compassion to all living creatures – not just human beings. This makes it consistent with ecological sustainability. It also chimes with the anti-consumerist ethos that is scornful of excess and superficiality.

Even if the number of westerners who subscribe to Buddhism is proportionally small, there are many more who have absorbed its key ideas. For example, the lotus is symbolically important for Buddhists because it reaches to the sun while having its roots in mud. The metaphor suggests we can attain spiritual maturity despite our material appetites – a doctrine of perfectibility that many today find cheering.

WHERE NEXT?

Anyone attracted to or intrigued by Buddhism will benefit from further immersion – listening to talks by some of the inspiring Buddhist sages, for example, or reading books by the Dalai Lama and others. However, with regard to enhancing happiness, there is no substitute for practical work:

- **Go on retreat** Withdrawing from everyday routines and comforts can nourish the spirit. The many types of retreat on offer may emphasize silence, simplicity, work or nature.
- **Take a meditation class** The sense of connection in a well-taught group is an additional benefit to the teaching expertise.
- **Explore Zen** Very different from Tibetan Buddhism, the Zen Buddhist tradition believes in encountering life directly, not through language or logic.

BUDDHISM IN A NUTSHELL
A REMINDER OF KEY PRINCIPLES

Committing to the relief of suffering.
Showing compassion.
Being selfless in the service of others.
The universal kinship of living things.
Mindfulness – stilling the 'monkey mind'.
Purity of thought, word and deed.
Regular meditation to train the mind.
Facing impermanence unflinchingly.
Cultivating the spirit.
Resisting fears and cravings.

'Radiate boundless love
towards the entire world.'

THE BUDDHA

FURTHER READING

Brown, Derren, *Happy: Why more or less everything is absolutely fine*, Bantam Press, London, 2006

Comte-Sponville, André, *A Short Treatise on the Great Virtues: The uses of philosophy in everyday life*, William Heinemann, London, 2002

Dalai Lama, The, and Howard C. Cutler, *The Art of Happiness: A handbook for living*, Riverhead, New York, 1998

Eagleton, Terry, *The Meaning of Life*, Oxford University Press, 2007

George, Mike, *Discover Inner Peace: The illustrated guide to personal enlightenment*, Duncan Baird Publishers, London, 2000

George, Mike, *Learn to Relax: Easing tension, conquering stress, freeing the self*, Duncan Baird Publishers, London, 1998

Kabat-Zinn, Jon, *Wherever You Go, There You Are: Mindfulness meditation for everyday life*, Piatkus, revised ed. 2004

Verni, Ken A. (consultant), *Practical Mindfulness: A step-by-step guide* (writer Mike Annesley), DK, London, 2015

Williams, Mark and Danny Penman, *Mindfulness: A practical guide to finding peace in a frantic world*, Piatkus, London, 2011

Hygge

Johansen, Signe, *How to Hygge: The secrets of Nordic living*, Bluebird, London, 2016

Wiking, Meik, *The Little Book of Hygge: The Danish way to live well*, Penguin, London, 2016

Positive psychology

Carr, Alan, *Positive Psychology: The science of happiness and human strengths*, Routledge, London, 2nd ed. 2011

Grenville-Cleave, Bridget, *Positive Psychology: A toolkit for happiness, purpose and well-being*, Icon Books, 2016

Seligman, Martin, *Authentic Happiness: Using the new positive psychology to realize your potential for lasting fulfilment*, Nicholas Brealey Publishing, London, 2011

Seligman, Martin, *Flourish: A new understanding of happiness and well-being – and how to achieve them*, Nicholas Brealey Publishing, London, 2011

Lykke

Wiking, Meik, *The Little Book of Lykke: Secrets of the world's happiest people*, Penguin, London, 2017

Ikigai

García, Héctor, and Francesc Miralles, *Ikigai: The Japanese secret to a long and happy life*, Hutchinson, London, 2017

Mogi, Ken, *The Little Book of Ikigai: The secret Japanese way to live a happy and long life*, Quercus, London, 2017

Lagom

Åkerström, Lola A., *Lagom: The Swedish secret of living well*, Headline Home, London, 2017

Dunne, Linnea, *Lagom: The Swedish art of balanced living*, Gaia, London, 2017

Buddhism

Dalai Lama, The, *The Little Book of Buddhism*, Rider, London, 2000

Hagen, Steve, *Buddhism Plain and Simple*, Penguin, London, 1999

Landaw, Jonathan, Stephan Bodian and Gudrun Bühnemann, *Buddhism for Dummies*, John Wiley & Sons, London, 2nd ed. 2011

INDEX

Ability 131
Acceptance 58. 94–95
Acquaintances 79, 98
Activity 13
Activity friendship 79
Aerobic exercise 24
Affection 72, 99
Affinity 101, 117
Affluenza 116
Afternoons 147
Ageing 26
Alertness 73
Altruism 67, 68
Ambition 58
Andersen, Hans Christian 63
Anxiety 72, 150
Apple 30
Appreciation 160
Aptitude 23
Aristotle 10, 14, 79, 93, 144
Artists 76
Asceticism 53
Aspirational 124
Authenticity 59, 69, 80–81
Autumn 50
Awareness 181
Balance 135, 142–3, 152, 167
Bathing 52
Beauty 163
Beliefs 59
Belonging 72, 124
Beltane 50
Berries 43
Betrayal 90, 91
Bicycle 55
Birds 48
Blake, William 144
Blame 127
Bodhisattva 182
Body 85, 151
Boxes 41
Breathing 181
Buddha, Siddhartha Gautama 170–2, 174, 179, 189

Buddhism 26, 41, 116, 168–89
Burma 173
Calendar 50, 61
Cambodia 173
Camus, Albert 152
Cardinal virtues 69
Careers 137
Carers 138
Casual friendship 79
Celebrations 60, 62, 63, 122
Celtic calendar 50
Celtic cycle 49
Ceremony 61
Challenges 85, 120, 125
Change 71, 81, 99, 117, 177
Chant 185
Children 137–8
China 173
Choices 102
Christmas 49
Churchill, Winston 71
Civic action 157
Colette 21
Comfort 36, 40, 56, 63, 107, 172
Commitment 91
Companionship 56, 98
Compassion 84, 85, 87, 104, 106–9, 117, 169, 177, 182, 188, 189
Compliments 175
Concentration 78, 181
Confidence 164–5, 167
Confucius 166
Connections 78, 128, 133
Contentment 81
Control 76
Conversation 61
Cooking 61
Courage 69, 103
Creativity 69, 115
Csikszentmihalyi, Mihaly 77
Curiosity 69
Cycling 55
Cynicism 91
Dalai Lama 20, 74, 170, 177, 188
Dass, Ram 187
Debt 132

Decluttering 147, 160
Denmark 35, 61, 88
Depression 78
Deservedness 159
Desires 176–7
Destiny 113, 123
Determination 125
Dharma wheel 170, 171
Diamond Way 173
Diet 82
Disability 103
Disappointment 91–3, 95, 96, 106, 150, 176
Distrust 90
Diversity 109
Donating 75
Driftwood 43
Early mornings 147
Eclipse 47
Ecology 39
Egotism 164, 178, 179
Elevenses 147
Embarrassment 73
Emerson, Ralph Waldo 90
Emotion 27, 59, 66, 81, 95, 106
Emotions 173
Empathy 85, 106–9, 117, 125
Employment 22
Energy 122, 133
Enlightenment 171, 184
Enthusiasm 69, 73
Equality 159
Equinox 50
Esteem 124
Ethnicity 103
Evenings 147
Evidence–based science 67
Excellence 131
Executive strengths 69
Exercise 82
Existence 170
Experiences 81, 109, 127, 129
Fabric 52
Facebook 78
Failing 66, 126–7, 139
Fairness 69, 85, 142–3, 158–9, 167
Faith 84, 129

Family 44, 73, 91, 121, 136, 137, 138, 139
Fears 189
Fertility 62
Festivals 49, 51, 61, 63
Fitness 124
Fjords 46
Flexibility 26, 69
Flow and immersion 67, 76–7, 85
Flowers 48
Focussing 31
Food and drink 39
Footpaths 54–5
Footsteps 54
Forgiveness 57, 69, 80, 85, 87, 93, 94, 96, 97, 117
Four noble truths 170
Four-leafed clover 121
Franklin, Benjamin 8
Freedom 102, 103
Friends 52, 58, 63, 73, 75, 91, 98, 121, 127, 133, 146
Friendship 44–5, 78, 79, 85, 101
Fromm, Erich 62
Frugality 142–3
Frustration 22
Fulfilment 66
Generosity, 63, 72, 90
Giving 75, 85, 182
Goals 70, 122, 123, 125, 126, 128, 134, 165
Goats 62
Golden Mean, the 144
Goleman, Daniel 66
Good life 67, 111
Goodness 14
Gratitude 69, 72, 73, 80, 81, 85, 151, 160, 182
Groups 133
Haiku 135
Hall, Dr. Kathleen A. 103
Hanh, Thich Naht 178
Happiness Research Institute 88
Harmony 84, 167
Healing 24
Health 62, 82, 124, 128
Hearth 32–63

Heartland 112
Helping 109, 121
Holmes, Oliver Wendell 40
Home 112, 137, 147, 154
Hope 69
Hopelessness 73
Hubbard, Elbert 127
Humility 69, 164
Humour 69
Hurt 94, 117, 150
Hygge 17, 32–63, 88, 142
Identity 59
Ikea 143
Ikigai (purpose) 17, 113, 118–39
Ill health 26
Imagination 97, 125, 131
Imbolc 50
Impermanence 189
Impulse 74
Independence 128
Indian Tantra 173
Indoors 48
Initiative 133
Injustice 158
Insects 48
Inspiration 76
Intimacy 111
Intuition 93, 177
James, Oliver 116
Japan 173
Japanese 119, 120
Japanese Tendai 173
Joy 73, 81, 91, 98, 103
Judgement 69
Jung, Carl 114, 186
Justice 158
Kamiya, Mieko 139
Karma 84, 174
Karuna 182
Kawahigashi, Hekigodo 135
Kerouac, Jack 163
Killing, The 42
Kindness 69, 72–5, 85, 87, 162, 175, 182–3
Kinship 84, 183, 189
Lagom 17, 145, 140–67
Lammas 50
Landscape 54
Leadership 69
Learning 66, 132

Index 191

Lethargy 73
Lifestyle 24, 143, 146
Light 38
Listening 109
Little Book of Ikigai 134
Little Book of Lykke 88
Lonely 75
Lotus 188
Love 14, 16, 62, 80, 91, 99, 111, 115, 117, 124, 151, 177, 183, 189
Love tokens 112
Loved ones 100, 137
Lucky almond 61
Lunch times 147
Lupercalia 62
Lykke 17, 86–117
Lyubomirsky, Sonja 74
Mabon 50
Mahayana 173
Mandala 186–7
Mantras 184–5
Maslow, Abraham 66, 124
Meals 60
Meaning 23, 129
Meditation 19, 28–31, 84, 115, 151, 154, 169, 171, 178–81, 188, 189
Meehl, Paul 66
Meteor 47
Midsummer 50, 61
Mind power 176
Mindfulness 19, 24, 28–31, 63, 71, 90, 95, 107, 114, 128, 134, 137, 139–48, 150, 154–5, 165, 177, 178–9, 188, 189
Mistakes 165
Moderation 142
Mogi, Ken 134
Money 87, 114–16, 117
Moon 47
Morals 69
Morgan, Charles L. 85, 117
Nature 46, 48, 63, 111, 115
Neighbour 75
Nervous breakdown 153
Nicomachean Ethics 14, 15
Night 47

Noble Eightfold Path 170
Northern Lights 46
Norway 42
Nostalgia 73
Nutrition 82
Opportunity 130
Optimism 66, 70–1, 85, 120, 129
Ostara 50
Outdoors 48
Pain 13, 176
Paley, Grace 53
Parents 73, 138
Partners and partnership 83, 85, 90, 99, 101, 137, 147
Patience 162
Peace 81, 84, 96–7, 173, 176–7, 178, 184, 188
Pebbles 43
Performance 76
Perseverance 70
Persistence 69
Personal motivation 121
Pessimism 70
Pleasure 13, 15, 23, 102, 132, 135, 160–1, 167, 172, 176, 177
Positive psychology 64–85, 113
Positivity 64–85
Possessions 87, 110–13, 117
Prajna 182
Prayer 84
Principles 59, 189
Profession 56
Promises 105
Prudence 69, 85, 166
Psyche 177
Psychology 64–85, 113
Pure Land 173
Purity 150–1, 189
Purpose 120, 121, 124, 128, 129–33, 139
Reading 83, 147
Rebalancing 147
Receiving 182
Recycling 148, 156

Regret 73, 165
Reincarnation 171, 174
Rejection 95
Relationships 56, 67, 80–1, 100–1
Repetition 30
Resilience 26, 66, 127
Responses 24, 88, 95, 107
Responsibility 20, 25, 104
Restraint 143
Retreat 188
Rilke, Rainer Maria 184
Risalamande 61
Romance 39
Rowling, J.K. 125
Rugs 40
Rumi 80
Russell, Bertrand 153
Sacred map 186
Samatha 180
Samhain 50
Scandinavia 46, 60
Seasonings 52
Seasons 49
Self-analysis 57
Self-assessment 69
Self-awareness 31, 139, 150, 165, 173
Self-belief 123
Self-care 82–3, 162
Self-consciousness 73
Self-control 144
Self-esteem 76, 165
Self-exposure 90
Self-fulfilment 67, 124
Self-help 67
Self-indulgence 160
Self-knowledge 164
Self-respect 144
Selflessness 183, 189
Seligman, Martin 66, 68, 69, 80
Senses 52
Sensuality 53
Separation 26
Sexuality 103
Sharing 61, 92, 127
Sideways move 130
Signposts 123, 125

Simplicity 146
Sincerity 59
Singing 184
Single mindedness 126
Skills 131, 154
Sky 47
Sleep 82–3
Smell 63
Smiling 175
Social 121, 156, 158
Social media 78, 133, 146
Solar calendar 51
Solstice 50
Sound power 184
Souvenirs 112
Speech, freedom of 104
Speeches 60–1
Spinoza, Baruch 160
Spirit and spirituality 69, 189
Spring 50
Sri Lanka 173
Sri Yantra 186
Stand, taking a 103
Stars 47
Strengths 68
Stress 24, 72, 78, 153, 154, 181, 186
Striving 58
Study 67
Suffering 170, 172, 189
Summer 50
Sunlight 82
Sutras 171
Sweaters 42
Sweden 141, 143, 145, 156
Tagore, Rabindranath 166
Talents 67, 130, 131, 134, 165
Talking 81
Taste 63
Teachers 73, 171
Temperance 69, 160–1
Tension 154
Thailand 173
Theravada 173
Thich Nhat Hanh 83
Thoreau, Henry 46, 54–5
Thoughtfulness 63, 75

Three-dimensional living 89
Three-pronged stress strategy 24
Tibet 173
Tibetan Buddhism 168–89
Time management 25, 26, 146–7
Tipping 75
Tolerance 57
Tolstoy, Leo 113
Touch 36, 63
Trauma 26
Treasury 113
Trust 72, 87, 90, 91–3, 117
Truth 59, 151, 165, 177
Understanding 59, 108–9
Unemployment 26
Unhappiness 27, 176, 178
Vajrayana 173
Victim 127
Vipassana 178
Virtues 67, 68, 85, 175
Vision 122, 129, 132
Vitality 73
Walking 54–55
Walpurgisnacht 51
Warmth 38–9, 44, 61, 63
Weaknesses 68–9
Wealth 116
Well-being 72, 74, 137, 139, 185
Whitman, Walt 53, 106
Wiking, Meik 88–9
Winter 50
Wisdom 129, 171, 178, 182
Woodland 54–5
Work 22, 23, 67, 101, 121, 136, 139, 154
World Happiness Report 10, 17, 35, 87, 88
World Tree 51
Wreath 43
Yggdrasil Day 51
Yoga 2, 84
Yule 51
Zen 173, 188

lycka
السعادة
ευτυχία
štěstí
felicità
felicidad
hamingju
आनन्दन
hạnh
kebahagiaan
laime
счастье
Glück
خوشی
срећа
šťastie
אושר
injabulo
खुशी
boldogság
furaha